WALLACE NEFF 1895-1982

WALLACE NEFF 1895–1982

*The Romance
of Regional
Architecture*

**HENNESSEY
+ INGALLS**
ART + ARCHITECTURE
B O O K S
**Santa Monica
1998**

Frontispiece
Wallace Neff and Airform Construction
circa 1941

Edited by Andrea P. A. Belloli

Designed by Sheila Levrant de Bretteville

Assisted by Jennifer Egger

Manufactured in the United States of America

Copyright © 1989 The Huntington Library

1151 Oxford Road

San Marino, California 91108

626/405-2100

Reprinted, with permission, August, 1998, by

Hennessey + Ingalls

1254 3rd Street Promenade

Santa Monica, California 90401

California Architecture and Architects, No. 15

Library of Congress Cataloging-in-Publication Data

Wallace Neff 1895-1982 : the romance of regional architecture.

     p.   cm. -- (California architecture and architects ; no. 15)

   Originally published: San Marino, Calif. : Huntington Library,
c1989

   "Collaborative work done in connection with an exhibition
presented by the Virginia Steele Scott Gallery at the Huntington
Library from May 6 through September 4, 1989"--P. 12.

   Includes bibliographical references (p. 140-141).

   ISBN 0-940512-13-0 (trade pbk.)

   1. Neff, Wallace, 1895-   --Criticism and interpretation.

2. Regionalism in architecture--California, Southern.   I. Neff,
Wallace, 1895-   II. Virginia Steele Scott Gallery.   III. Henry
E. Huntington Library and Art Gallery.   IV. Series.

[NA737.N37W35   1998]

  728'.092--dc21   98-28885

This publication and the exhibition on which it was based
were organized for the Huntington Library by
a committee including Jay Belloli, Charles Calvo,
Alson Clark, Jan Furey Muntz, and Stefanos Polyzoides.
The publication and exhibition were made possible
by grants from the National Endowment for
the Arts, Washington, D.C., a federal agency,
and the Pasadena Gallery of Contemporary Arts.

Unless otherwise indicated, all illustrated buildings are
by Wallace Neff and are (or were) located in California.

C O N T E N T S

FOREWORD

Jay Belloli

Wallace Neff is one of those talented architects whose work bridges the revivalist concerns of the nineteenth century and the International Style of the twentieth. Like a number of his significant contemporaries, he has not received proper recognition. Between 1900 and 1940 many of these architects expanded the traditional concern for site to create buildings appropriate to the history, geography, and climate of the regions in which they were located. Regionalist architects re-explored earlier American styles but also reinterpreted other traditions – such as the Spanish or Italian – that were suitable to the areas for which they designed buildings.

The architecture of early Spanish and Mexican California was appropriate to the area's temperate climate, particularly in the southern part of the state. Wallace Neff was one of the most imaginative practitioners of the so-called California style, the legatee of these influences. As much as his buildings revived forms and details from earlier centuries, they were created for the modern age. Such work was possible only because of the understanding that existed between the various artists and craftspeople involved: the architect who designed the structure and orchestrated the process by which it was completed; the artist who could produce a sketch or rendering that captured the spirit of the structure as well as its particulars; the draughtsmen who combined the comprehensiveness of the building's scheme with the most precise detail; and the contractors, craftspeople and workers who were able to carry out the instructions embodied in the drawings while understanding the building's unity.

8

The regional architect's belief in, or acceptance of, the validity of the historical forms he interpreted faded before the rise of the International Style. Postmodernism's irony and frequent lack of historical understanding obviously do not mark a return to earlier regional attitudes. When one looks at the quality of construction and detail of historicizing buildings being created now, one realizes that the craftsperson's proud acceptance of an individual role in making a building has broken down as well.

Museums too rarely present the visual art of architecture to the public and, when they do, often show the work of architects on a logical and unswerving path toward modernism and beyond. It is, however, the architects who capture the shared myths and spirit of a period whose work defines our built environment and most influences our lives. Los Angeles, more than any other city, seems to re-create itself in cycles, from the optimistic new Mediterranean style of the '20s, the even greater eclecticism of the '30s, and the positive futurism of the '50s to the knowing, temporary-seeming architecture of the present. In re-creating itself so rapidly, the city has risked losing its identity as well as some of its greatest glories. This publication is the third in a series developed by a team of architects, curators, and scholars intended to document the important early twentieth-century architecture of the region before it disappears. It is our hope that such work will continue so all of us can better understand the variety and richness of Southern California's architectural history.

PREFACE

Robert A. M. Stern

In 1904 Henry James visited California and found it a "wondrous realm [that] kept suggesting . . . a sort of prepared but unconscious and inexperienced Italy, the primitive *plate*, in perfect condition, but with the impression of History all yet to be made." Wallace Neff's generation, as if taking James at his word, gave form to that history, looking not only to Italy for inspiration but also to Spain and, indeed, the entire Mediterranean in an effort to bring together climate, landscape, and culture in an architecture that embodied real and imagined historical traditions. Given the glories of Southern California's climate and the architects' talent, the result was an architecture that came quite close to achieving, for a moment at least, a paradise on earth.

Neff was not a great architect in the textbook sense of the word, nor was he an ideologue of style. Rather, he was a talented pragmatist graced with a sure sense of composition and a refined sense of detail. He understood what needed to be done for both the good of his clients and the public realm, and he pursued these twin objectives with taste, finesse, and invention.

Though most of Neff's best-known buildings were inspired by Mediterranean architecture, he cast his net widely enough to include elements from French and English vernacular. Yet, from building to building, from site to site, Neff's interpretations of divergent stylistic sources always embraced the search for an appropriate architecture for Southern California. No one project stands out – it is rather the sum of Neff's work, taken as an idiom, which is greater than its parts.

Neff left us an architecture so suited to its place and, in general terms, to our

way of life that at first glance it hardly seems a deliberate undertaking of art at all, just fine houses, a vernacular. Indeed, its characteristic low, sweeping lines, sunswept stucco facades, and red mission-tile roofs seem as native to the California landscape and climate as the tightly enveloped shingled and clapboarded houses do to the less temperate landscape of New England.

I welcome, then, this opportunity to celebrate Wallace Neff and what his work stands for, not only to marvel at his skill in adapting styles, forms, and even programs to the possibilities and constraints of site, or even to celebrate his role in the creation of a regional style. In my mind Neff's work affirms that architecture, if it is to succeed in the public realm, must reflect more than the pragmatics of program or technology or the naïve translation of a literary theory into a compositional game. In my mind Neff's work affirms that architecture, to fulfill itself as a public art, must address a wide audience in a familiar language, a language that goes beyond the mere expression of an architect's personal taste to embody a narrative of place and tradition.

ACKNOWLEDGMENTS

Jay Belloli and Amy Meyers

This publication is the result of collaborative work done in connection with an exhibition presented by the Virginia Steele Scott Gallery at the Huntington Library from May 6 through September 4, 1989, the first museum exhibition to survey the architecture of Wallace Neff. Neff's son Wallace L. Neff has generously promised much of the architect's archive as a gift to the Huntington's growing collection of American architectural renderings, sketches, drawings, and photographs. The Huntington is most grateful to Mr. Neff for this donation. His belief in his father's legacy and his stewardship of his work have enabled research on the architect's career to move forward.

During planning and research stages, Alan Jutzi and Brita Mack of the Huntington Library's Rare Book Department were both supportive and helpful. Arthur Neff, another of Wallace Neff's sons, provided additional information and encouragement. We would like to recognize Berge Aran, Architecture Department, University of California, Los Angeles; David Gebhard, Architectural Drawing Collection, University Art Museum, University of California, Santa Barbara; Victor Ingrassia, Fine Arts Library, University of Southern California; and the Academy of Motion Picture Arts and Sciences for their assistance in locating and preparing reproductions for the exhibition and this publication. Architectural photographers Grey Crawford, Marvin Rand, and Julius Schulman also provided necessary materials for this book.

Andrea P. A. Belloli edited the publication, and we are grateful for her contribution. Sheila Levrant de Bretteville is responsible for the book's design. Guilland Sutherland, editor, Huntington Library Publications, was generous in her support and assistance. Robert

Schlosser, principal photographer at the Huntington, and his staff worked under time constraints to print photographs for the book and the exhibition. Peggy Bernal, Development and Communications Officer at the Huntington, provided crucial support in seeking the funding needed for this project. Finally, we are grateful to the National Endowment for the Arts, Washington, D.C., a Federal agency, and to the Pasadena Gallery of Contemporary Arts for the grants that made it possible to organize this survey of Wallace Neff's architectural career.

WALLACE NEFF

and the

CULTURE

of LOS ANGELES

Alson Clark

Since the turn of the twentieth century Los Angeles has passed through three major cultural eras, each of which has been reflected in its architecture. When the city first became important, its architects began to be recognized; by 1920 Southern California was seen as heir to a tradition more flexible than that of the East Coast, whose architectural legacy was English, specifically Georgian. The buildings of the Spanish period on the West Coast had been rudimentary yet noble, descended from a Mediterranean culture that seemed classic and romantic at the same time. Imaginative architects were able to adapt and flesh out this tradition for the modern world. During the next era in modern California, the era of technology of the 1930s through the early 1960s, the Mediterranean tradition was abandoned in favor of the International Style, then dominant all over the country. The city of Los Angeles was now seen as technologically advanced, the first large metropolis to be designed for the automobile age. It was also seen as a city without tradition, a place where the latest ideas were immediately welcome. Since the mid-1960s Los Angeles has been seen as the national pop culture capital; its glitzy irreverence is counted as one of its prized assets. The *Hollywood* sign (which originally read *Hollywoodland* and was designed to promote a real estate subdivision) has become a major monument. A building in the shape of a hot dog intended to promote the sale of hot dogs is ranked as a treasure. As far as single-family homes are concerned (the single-family house is the city's dominant residential building type), houses of the 1920s ostensibly designed in historic styles but actually designed to sell to people who had little knowledge of history are seen as an early manifestation of pop culture and therefore historic.

Wallace Neff was an important architect for so long that his work was significant in each of these cultural eras. Born in 1895 in La Mirada, California, on a ranch owned by his maternal grandfather, Andrew McNally, founder of the mapmaking firm of Rand McNally, he was brought up in Altadena, adjoining Pasadena, in the same grandfather's Victorian mansion, a house that included an exotic and ornate Turkish smoking saloon purchased at the 1893 Columbian Exposition in Chicago. Neff was practically nurtured on architectural eclecticism. In 1909 his entire family

15

Previous Page
Fig. 2
**Mr. and Mrs. King C. Gillette
Ranch House,**
*Calabasas, 1929,
view from patio.*

Fig. 3
**Ralph Adams Cram (1863–1942)
Saint Anne's Chapel,**
*Arlington Heights, Massachusetts,
circa 1910.*

Fig. 4
Mrs. Edwin D. Neff House,
*Santa Barbara, 1919,
living room.*

departed for Europe, where they lived until forced to return home at the outbreak of World War I. Neff attended boarding school in Switzerland, traveled, and studied drawing and painting in Munich; he also apprenticed in a Munich architect's office.

After his return to America Neff managed to enroll as an architecture student at MIT despite his spotty secondary education, having been admitted on the recommendation of the eclectic architect-medievalist Ralph Adams Cram, then head of the architecture program. MIT in 1915 was probably the least provincial environment the United States could offer an architecture student. Cram's curriculum changes, which made the school at once more practical and more romantic and de-emphasized the Beaux-Arts verities, were to Neff's liking. He was impressed by Cram's work, in particular by some small, simple chapels with a Mediterranean flavor, such as Saint Anne's in Arlington Heights, Massachusetts (fig. 3).[1]

In 1917 Neff again found his life disrupted by the war. America had entered the conflict, and he was forced to leave MIT and work in a Wilmington, California, shipyard. He liked shipbuilding, taking an evening course in naval architecture at the University of Southern California and staying in Wilmington for at least six months after the war was over. He had an engineering bent, applying for patents for an automobile altimeter and a self-sharpening pencil while still a student. This talent was to surface again during the era of architectural technology.

After the Wilmington job Neff, then twenty-four years old, decided not to return to MIT but to take advantage of his mother's request to build her a vacation house in Santa Barbara and then to work for the Frank Meline Company, a real estate, insurance, and speculative building firm with offices in several cities in the Los Angeles area. These developments emphasize the fact that Neff was no architectural purist. He designed his mother's little house (fig. 4) in a free English medieval style at the very time when the Mediterranean was all the rage. Its interior had an Arts and Crafts simplicity we associate with the turn-of-the-century designs of Charles F. A. Voysey. Neff's subsequent decision to design speculative houses instead of returning to school or apprenticing with an outstanding practitioner (both options being

Fig. 5
Myron Hunt (1868–1952)
Mrs. E. M. Fowler House,
Chino, 1915.

open) suggest that his love of architectural practice, manifest in the longer than fifty-year span of his career, was a love of the rough and tumble rather than of the intellectual heights of the profession.

Neff got his license in 1921 and opened an office in Pasadena in 1922. As it turned out, European experience and East Coast credentials were important in launching a practice in postwar Los Angeles. The now-famous Greene and Greene were MIT men as were important practitioners such as Myron Hunt and Reginald Johnson, both of whom had made the Grand Tour. The well-known Santa Barbara architect George Washington Smith had studied painting in Paris and spent time in Spain. The work of these architects of the California school was gaining national recognition just when Neff began his career. In an article published in *Architectural Forum* in 1923, Aymar Embury II, a distinguished East Coast architect and writer, observed: "The great value and beauty of this new California work has been instantly recognized by almost all our magazines, so that even to the Eastern architect the names of George Washington Smith, Reginald Johnson and Myron Hunt are as familiar through their recent work as that of Bertram Goodhue. . . . California may be said to have 'found itself' architecturally, a thing not yet true of the East."[2] Myron Hunt, who had practiced under the influence of the Arts and Crafts movement in Chicago, advanced the profession after his move to California in 1903 by appreciating the architectural potential of the simple adobes of Spain and Mexico. His 1906 courtyard beach house for Henry Huntington was unornamented as was his 1915 Fowler House in Chino (fig. 5). Hunt had undoubtedly read Herbert Croly's 1913 description of what the California house should be: "It is peculiarly fortunate that California possesses historical associations with the most complete embodiment of the classic spirit in domestic architecture, viz., the Italian villa and garden."[3] The Fowler House is a simple, modern embodiment of the Italian villa tradition. George Washington Smith, who had learned to appreciate unornamented Mediterranean vernacular buildings through a study of Cézanne's painting,[4] emphasized the Andalusian in his own 1916 Santa Barbara house. His second house of 1920 is looser; it has a corbeled second-story balcony characteristic of the houses of California's

19

Fig. 7
Edward Drummond
Libbey Stables,
Ojai, 1923,
rendering.

Fig. 8
Libbey Stables,
elevations.

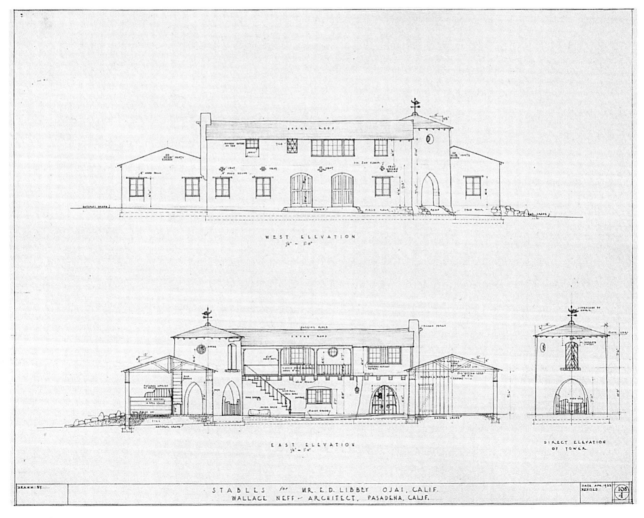

Fig. 9
Ojai Valley Country Club,
Ojai, 1923–24.

Mexican period up and down the coast (fig. 6).

In 1921 the editor of *Architect and Engineer of California*, Irving Morrow, started to use the term *Californian* to describe the eclectic style that was evolving in the state.[5] In 1913 Herbert Croly had labeled this style "a young and tender plant"; by 1928 A. Lawrence Kocher could report: "Out in the West steadily growing from year to year there has been developing an architectural entity. . . . It is unified. . . . It is not a personal manifestation. Individuals do not stand out above the crowd in the same way as they do in the East. . . . Furthermore it is not composed of just those building traditions that were inherited from the days of the Missions. . . . It would be difficult indeed and even impossible to separate what is native from what is borrowed."[6]

Neff began his career just as the California style was maturing; in fact, he always preferred to call his work Californian, a term that ceased to be applied after the modern movement supplanted the Mediterranean tradition. Neff became a leading practitioner in a remarkably short time. On April 10, 1923, the *Pasadena Star-News* reported that there was over $250,000 worth of work in the Neff office, "most in residences ranging from $15,000 to $30,000. . . . Mr. Neff has also completed plans for a clubhouse and stables in Ojai for E. D. Libbey of Toledo." These two commissions for an important client helped to make Neff's reputation. The stables (figs. 7, 8) are a tour de force; the adobe walls are left exposed (they had been chemically waterproofed), suggesting the scale and texture of stone; a corbeled balcony and a roof of hand-split wood shakes recall more strongly than George Washington Smith's 1920 house the adobe dwellings of the early Californians. Neff added a squat, circular tower suggesting a pigeon cote but not at the end of the building's main mass. As another attraction, strange, delicately pointed arches springing almost from the ground pierce the base of the tower and frame the front portal. Are these Saracenic or perhaps Gothic arches, and why were they employed on a building in the early California tradition? In the Ojai clubhouse (fig. 9) the proportions are horizontalized and the roof pitches dropped to two-and-a-half in twelve on the main roof and a mere two in twelve on the porches; in addition, the parapet railing of the exterior stair leading

Fig. 10
**Frances Marion and
Fred Thomson House,**
*Beverly Hills, 1923–24,
entrance with coats of arms.*

Fig. 11
Marion and Thomson House,
courtyard.

from the small second story is so plastic that it seems like lava flowing down a volcanic slope. Why did Neff force the design of a building supposed to be a re-creation of a Spanish adobe in this direction?

The answer to these questions, of course, is that Neff wanted and needed to establish his own manner of design. His approach appealed to a creative married couple in Hollywood, Frances Marion, a hugely successful scriptwriter, and her husband, Ben Thomson, a well-known (at the time) cowboy actor. Although in her autobiography *Off With Their Heads: A Serio-Comic Tale of Hollywood* (1972) Frances Marion refers to herself and her husband as "parvenus," they were aware and educated (he had an M.A. from Princeton). They commissioned a house from Neff (cover, figs. 10, 11). What they wanted was unusual, something that was impressive and yet thumbed its nose at convention in a nice way – imaginative, good-natured, whimsical grandeur, not mock impressiveness. The burlesque coat of arms the couple concocted that is modeled in low relief over the entrance is in the spirit of the place; it consists of a roll of film rampant over a horse's head and is emblazoned with a horseshoe for the good luck needed in Hollywood. The Thomson House is a light-hearted Mediterranean fantasy complete with its architect's curious elliptical arches inside and out, and with Oriental finials topping exotic round buttresses. Or are they columns or perhaps mock towers? (The motif reemerges at the rear of the house as curious paired chimneys.)

Neff's next major work was the Arthur K. Bourne House in San Marino (figs. 12, 13). Bourne was the playboy heir to a large fortune; Neff stated that he tried to endow the design with psychological overtones that would suggest Bourne's lifestyle, which was tasteful yet relaxed and pleasant.[7] The style of the Bourne House, purer Mediterranean vernacular than Neff's earlier designs, makes its details stand out dramatically. The horizontal main mass, fused to a lively circular tower at the left, is nearly free of openings except for a small recessed porch and a tiny central oval light. Such ovals are common in the farmhouses of Lombardy but not as central motifs. The Neff oval is surrounded by ebullient Spanish Colonial ornament recalling the more ornate motifs of Southwest missions. It seems to give the house an elegant stamp,

23

Fig. 12
**Mr. and Mrs.
Arthur K. Bourne House,**
San Marino, 1925, facade.

Fig. 13
Bourne House

Fig. 14
**Berkeley Avenue
Speculative House
for Lincoln Mortgage Company,**
San Marino, 1925.

being a shape associated with refinement. This mansion, visible from the street, occupies a double lot. From the first, when a model was exhibited in a real estate office during construction,[8] it attracted attention. Because its insouciant mood was admired, it became a favorite of the builders, who were enjoying a period of prosperity, for the population of Los Angeles was growing so fast that there was a severe housing shortage through most of the '20s.

As in other cities, builders supplied the great majority of housing in Los Angeles, but they had opportunities that were almost unique. First, the pervasive single-family house, sited on a wider-than-usual lot to allow access to the ubiquitous garage and for outdoor living in keeping with the area's delightful climate, posed a greater design challenge and also a greater design opportunity. Second, there was opportunity everywhere to create a new city on virgin land; very few traces had to be kicked over. When the development of Los Angeles had begun in the 1880s, builders had used East Coast designs; it was soon realized, however, that an opportunity was being lost in not acknowledging the area's own romantic past. The Mission Revival style began to be employed, often at the same time as the California bungalow form, which was used for more than a decade after the turn of the century. This latter house type, suited to the region, was made fashionable by Charles and Henry Greene in Pasadena. Their imaginative, luxurious creations aroused the interest of the public, and builders hastened to offer smaller and much less costly models that strove to retain the ambience of the originals. Much the same process occurred during the early '20s, only now it was the creations of architects who had worked in the Mediterranean tradition that caught the public's and builders' fancy. There were problems, however; a stucco-clad house, no matter how simple – or perhaps because it *was* so simple – needed a designer's touch to make it attractive and desirable. The only surviving Neff scheme for a very early speculative house, a perspective drawing for a relatively expensive model done during his days with the Frank Meline Company, was more than a little influenced by George Washington Smith's 1916 house in Santa Barbara. Smith's second house, too, was popular with builders. Its front door was set at a forty-five-degree angle, and builders felt that a

25

Fig. 15
Tract House,
Los Angeles,
circa 1927.

Fig. 16
Imitation Bourne House,
Beverly Hills, 1929,
Vance Wallin, builder and owner.

door set at a forty-five-degree angle was just the thing for a corner lot, so this house occurred on corner lots all over the region.

After Neff began his practice he designed straightforward houses in a tract for the Lincoln Mortgage Company (fig. 14) beginning in 1924. After 1925 he was too busy to participate in the design of tracts, although he did design individual spec houses for family members. Speculative builders loved the vivacity of Neff's work and unashamedly copied it (fig. 15). As observed at the time, much of the "Super-Spanish" tract house architecture from the '20s in Los Angeles looks the way it does because of Neff. Writing in 1927, Harris Allen, editor of *Pacific Coast Architect*, described Neff's "extraordinary vogue – one can call it nothing less . . . so that people exclaim, 'There is another Neff house,' as they drive by. . . . Some characteristic features have been seized upon and reproduced with a frequency that is somewhat disconcerting, if flattering."[9] Another observer, M. Urmy Seares, editor of *California Southland*, wrote in 1926, "In so short a time his original work has been the inspiration of countless copyists."[10] The prominent architect H. Roy Kelley had this to say: "Wallace Neff did a very interesting house with a circular entrance motif, well-proportioned and the house was large enough to stand it. Within six months the landscape was infested with miniature bungalows all designed in the silo-Spanish style and paying court to the round house."[11]

Sometimes entire compositions were lifted, as in the Beverly Hills house of 1929 that is the Bourne House reversed (fig. 16). An even more remarkable example of plagiarism is the 1929 house on Los Feliz Boulevard, where the front elevation of Neff's 1924 Henry W. Schultz House, much published at the time, was copied closely (figs. 17, 18). Other designers such as Wilmer J. Hersey in the Pasadena area and David Malcolm Mason on the west side of Los Angeles aped Neff's "soft" stucco surfaces in compositions less closely identified with his designs. It was Seares's "countless copyists" who made Neff's vocabulary – the egg-shaped arch, silo tower, corbeled balcony running partway across the facade, horizontal stress, and overly low roof pitch – so ubiquitous that Los Angeles would hardly be Los Angeles without them. Even on small houses a number of these features were crammed in, set off by a confusion of skyrocketlike bursting palms, leafy

27

Fig. 17
**Mr. and Mrs.
Henry W. Schultz House,**
San Marino, 1924.

Fig. 18
Imitation Schultz House,
Los Angeles, 1929.

Fig. 19
**Mr. and Mrs.
Parker Toms House,**
San Marino, 1924.

banana plants, and birds of paradise (the "official" flower of Los Angeles). The frantic results recall the pace of the '20s; Neff's tranquil hedonism, evoking the resort character of Pasadena or Beverly Hills, which *were* resort towns in those days, had been lost. What remained, perhaps, was his characteristic ambiguity; the houses are daring in some respects, yet they hanker for the past. They reflect the city's ambivalent self-image, its bifurcated culture.

There is no doubt that the slight kitsch aura of Neff's early work is what causes it to be admired in today's pop culture Los Angeles. Charles Moore prefers Neff's 1924 Toms House in San Marino (fig. 19) to the George Washington Smith house across the street[12] and calls the nearby Bourne House "one of the most satisfying examples of the Spanish-Colonial Revival ever built."[13] Neff's vivacity and his refusal to take himself too seriously are part and parcel of the postmodern sensibility.

After 1925 the architect's work gained in maturity. The Fred Niblo House of 1926 (figs. 20-22) and the Berg House of 1928, for example, have fascinating plans, both built around circular motor courts, but the elevations are more sober, more restrained than the early work. The great 1929 ranch house for King Gillette, inventor of the safety razor, recalls a Mediterranean village, perhaps a desert village in North Africa, but the means employed to suggest romance are simpler than before; the elliptical arch, for instance, was used only once (fig. 2). In Neff's own much-acclaimed house of 1928, it is not used at all (figs. 23, 24).

When the Depression struck, Neff, left with little work, tried to maintain momentum with an imaginative scheme for a mobile home, but the market was not ready for it. After his move to Hollywood, where he lived and worked until his retirement forty years later, his practice resumed. As Los Angeles entered the technological era, Neff worked on his concept of the Airform or Bubble House, a wonderfully simple scheme that was to provide good shelter for masses of people, mostly in the third world, during the '40s and '50s. This invention made Neff persona grata with the

29

Fig. 20
Fred Niblo House,
Beverly Hills, 1926,
sections and plot plan, detail,
drawn by Arthur E. Fisk.

Fig. 21
Niblo House,
elevations, drawn by
Clifton R. Hoskins.

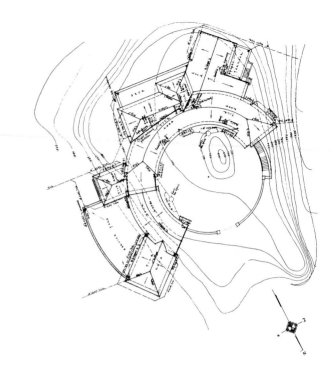

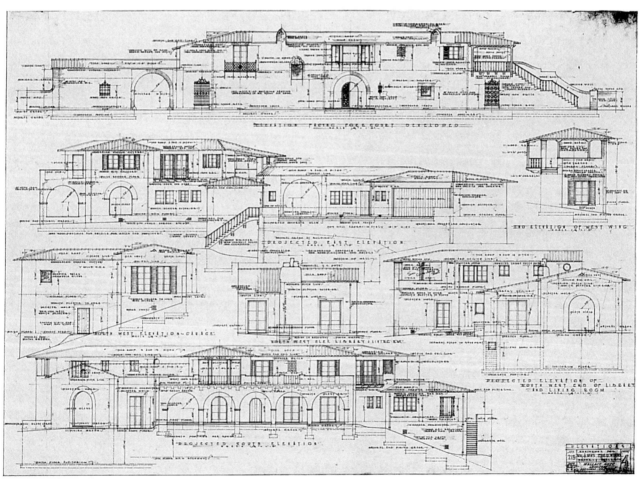

Fig. 22
Niblo House.

modernist establishment that dominated architecture at the time. Articles on the Bubble House appeared in professional journals in Europe and Latin America, of which the acclaimed Neff made a sort of triumphal tour in 1947.

As soon as houses that were rigorously modern and ascetic began to become less than fashionable in the early '60s, the *haute bourgeoisie* of Los Angeles began to cast longing glances at buildings of the recent past and to ask, "Who did that wonderful house?" The answer was often Wallace Neff. When the architect brought out a book on his own work in 1964, everyone recognized that he was still available, and he ended his career by doing some of his best work since the '20s and '30s. The informal brick-clad Roy Eaton House of 1962 (fig. 25) is a more modest variant of the grand Edward L. Doheny Ranch of 1929; the Singleton House in Holmby Hills is a very large version of the house Neff had done for the film star Joan Bennett in 1938. It was a good way to end a very long career that spanned three cultural epochs in the history of Los Angeles.

Fig. 23
**Mr. and Mrs.
E. Wallace Neff House,**
San Marino, 1928.

Fig. 24
Wallace Neff House,
*view from living room
into north patio.*

Fig. 25
Roy and Dorothy Eaton House,
Santa Barbara, 1962.

Notes

1. Conversation with Wallace Neff, March 1978.

2. Aymar Embury II, "Modern American Country Houses," *Architectural Forum* 38 (March 1923), p. 79.

3. Herbert Croly, "The Country House in California," *Architectural Record* 34 (December 1913), p. 485.

4. David Gebhard, *George Washington Smith*, exh. cat. (Art Galleries, University of California, Santa Barbara, 1964), p. 12.

5. Irving F. Morrow, "A New Bank in Santa Barbara," *Architect and Engineer* 64 (August 1921), p. 117.

6. A. Lawrence Kocher, "The American Country House," *Architectural Record* 58 (November 1928), p. 407.

7. Conversation with Wallace Neff, March 1978.

8. "A New House on Lombardy Road," *California Southland* 7 (October 1925), p. 22.

9. Harris Allen, "Adventures in Architecture," *Pacific Coast Architect* 32 (September 1927), p. 9.

10. M. Urmy Seares, "The California House in Florida," *California Southland* 7 (September 1926), p. 8.

11. H. Roy Kelley, "The California Situation from the Architect's Point of View," *Pacific Coast Architect* 33 (November 1928), p. 11.

12. Charles Moore, Peter Becker, and Regula Campbell, *The City Observed: Los Angeles* (New York, 1984), p. 345.

13. Ibid.

REGIONALISM

and

ROMANCE

David Gebhard

In 1927, at the height of the period revivals in America, the Beaux-Arts-educated architect Harry F. Cunningham lamented the "insipid sameness that has made America so easy to 'see' without leaving home."[1] Cunningham attributed the cause of this sameness to the universality of the "marvelous movies – the printed picture – the faithful flivver. Ours is a 'syndicated civilization' – why bother with 'regional' types?"[2] Certainly, one of the exhilarating battlegrounds of American architecture in this century has been the conflict between national, and even internationalist, images and regional ones.

Within the continental United States varied Hispanic modes repeatedly have been seized upon to create illusions of regionalism – whether on the Florida coasts, within the greater Southwest from Texas to Arizona, or along the Pacific coast of California. Always, though, these efforts at cultivating regional forms (ranging from city plans to gardens to groups of buildings or individual ones) have been countered by a pull on planners, landscape architects, architects, and, above all, clients to participate in fashions of the moment derived from the international or national scene.

Equally distressing for the advocates of regionalism has been their inability to contain specific images within geographical boundaries. Once a regional image such as California's Mission Revival style of the turn of the century had begun to transform Los Angeles or Riverside, it inevitably leaked out of its regional boundaries and cropped up in some of the least likely locales across the country. Ironically enough, a number of these "impossible" transplants were designed by one or another of the principal proponents of geographic regionalism. Arthur B. Benton, the designer of California's great monument of the Mission style, the Mission Inn in Riverside (1902 and later; fig. 26) apparently experienced no qualms about using the same style for a recreation building (1905) in Loring Park in Minneapolis. Irving J. Gill, California's most eloquent abstractor of the mission image, produced his most flamboyant Missionesque design for the Ellen Mason House (1902) in faraway Newport, Rhode Island.[3] Casualness, or perhaps the insistent demands of clients, prompted Pasadena architects Reginald D. Johnson, Gordon Kaufmann, and Roland Coate to plunk down a Spanish-image dwelling in suburban Winnetka,

Previous Page
Fig. 26
**Arthur B. Benton
(1859–1927),
Myron Hunt, and others,**
Mission Inn, Riverside, 1902–

Fig. 27
**Reginald Johnson (1882–1952),
Gordon Kaufmann (1888–1949),
and Roland Coate (1892–1958),
F. P. Warren House,**
*Winnetka, Illinois,
1922, entrance.*

Fig. 28
**Irving Gill (1870–1936),
Clark House,**
Santa Fe Springs, 1919–23.

Illinois, for F. P. Warren (1922) (fig. 27). At the end of the 1920s George Washington Smith, California's acknowledged master of the Spanish, provided Charles Cheney with a classic Andalusian farmhouse on the Atlantic shore of Fisher's Island (1929).

While Harry Cunningham argued that the public and individual clients made it impossible effectively to establish regional types, a closer look indicates that much of the gamesmanship of regionalism versus nationalism was due to the architects themselves. In the case of Benton, well over two-thirds of his California buildings were non-mission inspired, ranging from his own late version of the Shingle style to the English Tudor mode and the California bungalow. Even Gill, who was ideologically firm in his commitments to his "Cubist" version of the Mission style, continually absorbed the latest fashions. His 1919–23 Clark House in Santa Fe Springs has strong references to both Pre-Columbian architecture and the northern Italian villa (fig. 28). In his late work of the 1920s and early 1930s he absorbed elements of then-fashionable Art Deco.

The richest time for this play of contradictions in California occurred during the 1920s and '30s. These were the years when California, and especially Southern California, was attempting to convey its specialness, its marked difference from other areas of the country. The source of imagery for this new phase of regionalism was not really the Spanish and Mexican period of the late eighteenth and early nineteenth centuries but (like other period revival styles of the time) looked directly to Europe for its inspiration. "Since Italy and Spain have an all-year outdoor climate with prevailing wind similar to that of southern California," wrote Reginald D. Johnson in 1923, "the Mediterranean inspiration seems to be a logical one for this part of the country."[4]

By the end of the '20s Johnson himself had emerged as one of California's principal proponents of the Mediterranean image. Yet, during these same years (and later) he produced other period revival images – American Colonial, French eighteenth-century, English Tudor – all of which were national, or nonregional, in character. What was true for Johnson was equally true for others who were generally thought of as proponents of the Mediterranean:

Fig. 29
**Dr. and Mrs. Phillip
Schuyler Doane House,**
San Marino, 1924.

Fig. 30
Pickfair renovation,
Beverly Hills, 1926 – 34.

George Washington Smith of Santa Barbara, William Templeton Johnson and Richard Requa of San Diego, and Myron Hunt, Carleton M. Winslow, John Byers, Gordon Kaufmann, and Roland Coate of Los Angeles.

California, and especially Southern California, had an advantage over other regions of the country: its ability fully to maneuver the landscape to mirror the architectural image. The regional argument – Mission, Spanish, Mediterranean, or whatever it might be – was sustained to a considerable degree by the illusion of landscape. Equally, any one of the national or international images – English Cotswold cottage, French Norman farmhouse, or New England Colonial – could not be set down in an appropriate historic/geographic landscape.

The complexities inherent in this larger dilemma are illustrated in the designs of Wallace Neff. By 1927 he was being referred to as "one of the most brilliant proponents in the West of the 'Mediterranean style.'"[5] The San Francisco architect and writer Harris Allen called him an "Artist in Adobe," and though he was quite young at the time, Neff's name was often coupled with those of Smith, Johnson, and others as a "passionate" advocate of California's developing regional Hispanic/Mediterranean style.[6] Yet Neff, like his California colleagues, was at the same time producing a broad array of other period revival designs whose reference points were international/national, not regional.

Neff's gambrel-roofed, loosely medieval hillside cottage for his mother in Santa Barbara completely ignored any hint of California's Hispanic/Mediterranean-ism. By the mid–1920s he had sallied forth into English and French medieval styles then popular nationally. His 1924 Phillip Schuyler Doane House in Pasadena (fig. 29), along with his Hall House in San Marino of 1925, are French Norman. These were matched by exercises in the Tudor, including Pickfair, the Mary Pickford/Douglas Fairbanks house in Beverly Hills (1925; fig. 30), and others.

By the end of the 1920s Neff's Mediterranean predilections had caused him to turn to the image of the Tuscan villa. In these designs he could still pose as the regionalist, but now the formula was more "correct" and formal. During the decade of the Depression Neff

abandoned any pretense of advocating California regionalism. He did continue to design Hispanic-image dwellings, including the Mexican-inspired Amelita Galli-Curci House in Westwood (1936; fig. 31) and his version of a modernized California ranch house for Mr. and Mrs. King Vidor in Beverly Hills (1937; fig. 32). A majority of these schemes mirror what was popular on the national scene (though interestingly enough, Neff never took up any version of the Anglo Colonial, an image dominant throughout the country, including in California, nor did he embrace California's own colonial image, Monterey Revival).

With the exception of a small contingent of Southern California architects led by Cliff May and others, Neff's fellow practitioners pursued a similar course – from advocacy of Hispanic/Mediterranean regionalism in the '20s to national/ international period revivalism or modernism in the following decade. Neff's selection of images really had little to do, then, with any broad conceptual view he might have entertained about California and its relation to the rest of the country. He was adroitly keeping his eye directed toward what really mattered, changes in current fashion.

Images (or "types") are the varied languages of architecture; what one does with them, and what one may contribute to them, is what differentiates the work of one architect from another. Rexford Newcomb posed the question of individual personality in Neff's work in a 1926 article, "Personality in Regional Architecture."[7] Newcomb attributed Neff's "charming mannerism" to "a certain graceful, flowing plasticity."[8] In 1924 Harris Allen had spoken of Neff's "rather sheer creative joy in modeling a plastic material into form."[9] Both Newcomb and Harris were thinking primarily of the architect's stucco-walled Spanish/Mediterranean buildings, though they and others were well aware that a "Neffish" atmosphere was present in all of his images.

What was this "Neffish" quality which Allen occasionally found "a little too much in evidence"?[10] As with the majority of architects and clients of the '20s and '30s, there was an overall desire to immerse oneself in some romantically conceived episode of the distant past or to be magically transported to some exotic, faraway place. The Saint Louis architect

Fig. 33
**Douglas Fairbanks and
Marguerite de la Motte
in "The Mark of Zorro,"**
1920.

Fig. 34
**Horace M. Dobbins
Hillside Development Project,**
Pasadena, 1924, rendering.

Louis La Beaume beautifully captured this view of his age when he wrote,

> *Evidence of the sordidness, the seriousness, the steadying business of life are all about us in woeful abundance; and we seek escape*
> *from the real world . . . into a world of dreams. We long to turn our backs on our rigid, grimy warehouses, on the geometric hives we*
> *call offices, on the harshly efficient plants where so many of our working hours are spent, and fly for solace to Fairyland. Fairyland*
> *lies somewhere out near the edge of the city or beyond it, and is a place of enchanted houses and gardens. Hansel and Gretel, Red*
> *Olaf, Guy the Crusader, Don Quixote or Peleas and Melisande might be watching us from the windows.*[11]

In a delightfully open fashion La Beaume argued that what was needed was not adult sophistication and seriousness but a cultivated continuation of the "romanticism of adolescence." When successfully carried out in a period revival house and its garden, this romanticism could fully realize itself. It was this atmosphere – the romanticism of the child – which underlay Neff's domestic designs of the '20s and later.

But there is a quality inherent in Neff's expression of "adolescent romanticism" that sets his designs apart from those of other practitioners on the Southern California scene. It was this quality that strongly appealed to his clients and at the same time evoked reservations about his designs on the part of critics and other architects. It has little to do with the historic image employed and is closely bound up with Hollywood films.

As we have already seen, Harry F. Cunningham had (to put it mildly) grave reservations about the effect of popular films. "These movies have much to do," he wrote, "with public taste (or the lack of it)."[12] His elitist disdain for popular culture was shared by most of the "serious" architects of the time. Countering this view were many of those involved with the film industry, the clients, in many cases, of Neff and others. Cecil B. DeMille was as strident in his belief in the benefits of film in improving public taste as he was creatively exuberant in the films he directed: "As the most

Fig. 35
Dr. Walter Jarvis Barlow House,
Sierra Madre, 1925.

pervasive influence . . . motion pictures have had a definite influence upon trends taken by architecture within the past decade; . . . I would say clearly that Motion Pictures have more to do with Architecture than the layman and architect realize."[13] DeMille concluded by observing that "[o]f course California types [of architecture] have been particularly fortunate in this respect because so many pictures are made here."[14]

Here, perhaps, we have a clue to the quality that set Neff's work off from that of his California colleagues. His childlike, romantic images of the past were not directly inspired by tales and drawings encountered in books, nor were they simply enlargements of dollhouses. His vision was through the popular medium of film; his gardens and buildings were intended to be experienced as one would a Hollywood set (figs. 33, 34). Such an approach was nontraditional, pulling the design ever farther away from the accepted "reality" of architecture. It was this mysterious quality, as Harris Allen observed, that offended "the student of tradition, the advocate of restraint and subtlety."[15]

As with "the marvelous movies – the printed picture – the faithful flivver," Neff's designs were essentially populist. Like the Hollywood film they succeeded by exaggeration of sentiment; not the child-derived sentiment that Louis La Beaume was thinking of but the exaggerated portrayal of sentiment associated with the stage and film. Neff's exaggerated arches, his flowing, plastic treatment of surfaces, and his fondness for pressing buildings excessively into the ground are but a few of the design devices he manipulated to emphasize sentiment dramatically. The individual historic image, whether Andalusian Spanish, Tuscan (figs. 35, 36), or French Norman, was merely a means to an end. That his approach was highly successful is attested to by his many clients, the continual affirmative reaction of the press, and, finally, our own response today, when his language of exaggerated sentiment seems as potent as it did in the '20s and '30s.

47

Fig. 36
**Mr. and Mrs.
King C. Gillette Ranch House,**
Calabasas, 1929.

Notes

1. Harry F. Cunningham, "The Sameness of American Architecture," *American Architect* 131 (January 5, 1927), p. 13.

2. Ibid.

3. Rose Standish Nichols, "A Newport House and Garden," *House and Garden* 7 (April 1905), pp. 189–194.

4. Boardman Pickett, "The Influence of Climate on California Country Homes," *Country Life* 44 (October 1923), p. 52.

5. Charles Ray Glass, "The Return of the Spanish Hacienda," *Arts and Decoration* 30 (January 1927), p. 40.

6. Harris Allen, "An Artist in Adobe," *Pacific Coast Architect* 26 (August 1924), pp. 5–6, 17.

7. Rexford Newcomb, "Personality in Regional Architecture," *Western Architect* 35 (February 1926), pp. 22–23.

8. Ibid., p. 23.

9. Allen (note 6), p. 5.

10. Harris Allen, "Adventures in Architecture," *Pacific Coast Architect* 32 (September 1927), p. 9.

11. Louis La Beaume, "The Picturesque," *Journal of the American Institute of Architects* 16 (September 1928), p. 345.

12. Cunningham (note 1), p. 13.

13. Cecil B. DeMille, "Motion Pictures and Architecture," *Bulletin, Allied Architects Association of Los Angeles* 1 (July 1, 1925), n.p.

14. Ibid.

15. Allen (note 10), p. 9.

Fig. 37
**Mr. and Mrs.
George O. Noble House,**
Pasadena, 1927.

NEFF and NEUTRA:

REGIONALISM

VERSUS

INTERNATIONALISM

James F. O'Gorman

Two substantial houses erected on hilly sites in the Los Angeles area at the same moment exemplify polemical positions in the architectural situation of the 1920s and '30s. They are Wallace Neff's house for the George O. Nobles on Burleigh Drive in Pasadena (1927; fig. 37) and Richard Neutra's house for Gertrude and Philip Lovell on Dundee Drive in Los Feliz (1927–29; fig. 38). The latter is the premier early example of International Style modernism; the former, among the finest of Neff's regional "Californian" works. The dichotomy between them represents in microcosm the spectrum of early twentieth-century American architecture.[1]

The Lovell House is, of course, a "chestnut" of the history of modern design. It was broadly analyzed and generally praised even before its appearance in an exhibition held in 1932 at New York's Museum of Modern Art, an institution dedicated to promoting European modernism in America. The catalogue of that exhibition, Henry-Russell Hitchcock and Philip Johnson's *International Style*, became the "blue book" of the modern movement. The house fit perfectly into the "single new style" the authors defined as volumetric rather than massive, regular rather than axial, and devoid of "arbitrary applied decoration" (they left to others the addition of a moral dimension). The first two characteristics were generated by the structural frame, the armature of the new made possible by innovations in technology and materials during the nineteenth century. For Hitchcock and Johnson, as for the designers whom they catalogued, the frame was primary: it was, a priori, the fact of modern architecture to which all other considerations, including use, were secondary. "Thus technically the prime architectural problem of distribution is to adjust the irregular and unequal demands of function to regular construction and the use of standardized parts," they wrote.[2] In other words, to paraphrase Louis Sullivan's aphorism, form followed frame.

"The frame *was* the house; the house *was* the frame," Thomas Hines has written of Neutra's Lovell design. "[S]tructurally and aesthetically, it gave the house its meaning."[3] Neutra later made it sound as if the sloping plot had dictated his design,[4] but in fact, this European-born designer brought the concept of the frame to the hillside and might have employed it on

Fig. 38
Richard Neutra (1892–1970),
Gertrude and Philip Lovell House,
Los Angeles, 1927–29.

Fig. 39
Richard Neutra,
Lovell House,
living area.

any piece of land.[5] The house appears to float above, rather than sit upon, its terraced site. This "first completely steel-framed residence in America" was the product of the latest technology, with prefabricated elements bolted together, open web ceiling and floor joists, stock steel casements, and walls of Gunite shot onto wire.[6] The framed box imposes its measure on the patterns of life. Interior spaces are the "leftovers" of a process that began not with use but with concept.[7] The frame created them;[8] they did not result from convenience, comfort, or other creature considerations. For example, the library is a corridorlike space, low, long, and narrow. The flat-ceilinged living area is a larger rectangular tunnel shaped by the three-dimensional grid (the oft-printed early photograph looking from the library into the living area was taken from a low tripod and suggests an interior taller and broader than it is [fig. 39]).[9] The traditional stone fireplace looks out of place in such a conceptual framework. Everywhere in the Lovell House the dogma of modernism expressed through the medium of the three-dimensional steel structure dominates patterns of use. The house became a paradigmatic emblem of the new by the application of the implacable platonic gridwork of internationalism.

In Hitchcock and Johnson's catalogue the Lovell House joined similar buildings of all types from across the western world to form a coherent style conforming to three simple rules, none of which related to location. Such a universally applied aesthetic stood in direct opposition to a strong current of regionalism that existed in this country during the early twentieth century, a current exemplified in architectural design by the best work of Wallace Neff between 1919 and 1931. Neff's Noble House is a technically traditional, massively walled structure that molds itself to the contours of its hilltop site and assumes the generic mantle of the Spanish Revival style. The hub of the plan is the circular entrance and stair hall in the angle between the living and dining wings (fig. 40). One axis spreads out to the right (through the library) and left (through the living room and loggia) toward the distant San Gabriel Mountains, while a cross-axis leads forward onto an airy, round-arched loggia. Geo-metric extensions of the building – driveway, gardens, and terraces – as well as the service wing

Fig. 40
**Mr. and Mrs.
George O. Noble House,**
Pasadena, 1927, entrance hall.

Fig. 41
**George Washington Smith,
Osthoff House,**
Pasadena, 1924.

tumble downhill from this central vantage point. Interior spaces are variously shaped in anticipation of human ceremony, convenience, and visual delight. For example, the central, spiraling stair gives access to a broad, vaulted passageway leading to the bedrooms. The master bedroom has two sets of French doors, a quarter-round fireplace that nestles easily into the corner between them, and a ceiling coved so slightly that it is more felt than seen as giving lift and life to the space. All of this is ultimately made possible by flexible planning and the malleability of stuccoed brick walls, round-arched openings, low-pitched red-tile roofs, and a picturesque skyline of variously placed gables and chimneys – the latter part of the vocabulary of what had come to be known as the Californian look. In other words, form followed style.

Neff in the Noble House joined a host of designers from California across the Southwest to Florida who had been working since just before the turn of the century in Mission, Mediterranean, Pueblo, or Spanish Revival styles or combinations thereof. From the '10s through the '30s Rexford Newcomb defined, chronicled, and illustrated various aspects and examples of this regional architecture.[10] "California, and recently Florida," he wrote in 1928 about the work of Neff, George Washington Smith (fig. 41), Reginald D. Johnson, and other Southland designers, "capitalized upon her history, romance and lore with the result that her architecture speaks more eloquently of her glorious present and colorful past than does any other phase of her artistic expression."[11] Newcomb and other writers of the period championed an architectural style or styles based on the idea that Southern California possessed an agreed-upon regional culture descended from Spanish and Mexican roots[12] and promoted the work of architects such as Neff who could provide works that reflected that heritage.

The Lovell and Noble houses stemmed from given systems of architectural design. In the 1920s neither was alone of its kind. The preconceptual frame of Neutra's house and the preconceptual style of Neff's residence joined domestic works by these and other designers to shape the architectural scene in California. Rudolf M. Schindler's Newport Beach house for the Lovells (1925–26; fig. 42), "a doctrinaire assertion of the new architecture"[13] by another

Fig. 42
Rudolf M. Schindler (1887–1953),
Lovell Beach House,
Newport Beach, 1925–26.

Fig. 43
**Mr. and Mrs.
Clark B. Millikan House,**
Pasadena, 1931.

European-born designer, was conceived as a series of five parallel concrete frames that elevate and shape the enclosed rectangular volumes. Neff's Clark B. Millikan House of 1931 (fig. 43), located in Flintridge, on the other hand, drapes itself over its site on a plan that is formal and flexible at the same time. A central, hilltop entrance patio gives access to a service wing to the left, living area ahead, and sleeping rooms to the right, all of which plunge down over the crest of the rise as red- and blue-trimmed, white-walled, tile-roofed, arch-opened, and chimney-spiked Hispanic forms (figs. 44, 45).

From Sheldon Cheney[14] to David Gebhard,[15] critics and historians of California's domestic architecture of the early twentieth century, while noting the differences, have also remarked on the continuities between modernism and the Hispanic styles that resulted largely from shared simplicity and chromatics; tersely put, both in general favored untextured white walls. Recognition of this superficial continuity must be offset by a perception of such fundamental distinctions as the up-to-date technological symbolism that underlies the one and the traditional handmade aesthetics of the other. This is a distinction between the cerebral, sharp-edged, evenly illuminated, apparently weightless, two-dimensional planes of modernism versus the optical manipulation of light and shadow patterns cast on heavy walls by beam ends, wrought iron, tiled eaves, and "other scenic devices" (to quote Newcomb again[16]) characteristic of Hispanic forms. The one is best revealed by fluorescent lamps, whereas Newcomb happily dubbed the other a "sun-begotten style." Emphasis on the continuity between works such as these by Neutra and Neff not only obscures the visually obvious; it dilutes the polemic they represented in the era between the two world wars and thereby impoverishes the richness of recent architectural history.

A nation of voluntary and forced immigrants is nervous about its identity. The shape of American architecture is a design problem that has concerned American practitioners and critics at least since the Civil War. By the early twentieth century there were those who thought that while a truly national style was probably impossible, given the vastness and diversity of the country, a collection of regional styles might at least identify that characteristic

Fig. 44
Millikan House,
living room.

Fig. 45
Millikan House,
aerial view.

diversity. In a brief note on Neff's work published in 1926, for example, that leading proponent of regionalism Rexford Newcomb wrote: "[I]n a great country like our own it would seem folly to seek an homogeneous architectural expression. . . . [This is] impossible for several reasons among the chiefest of which are: the great varieties of topography, geology and climate . . . , and the wide diversity of historic and ethnic backgrounds of our people."[17] Colonial and Federal revivals in New England and along the Atlantic coast, picturesque fieldstone farmhouses in Pennsylvania, Prairie School houses in the Midwest, Hispanic, or at least Mediterranean, forms from Florida through the Southwest to California: these and other styles were rooted in local historical or physical characteristics. By the 1920s the Californian was one among many established American regional styles; against such indigenous diversity, the International Style must have appeared a homogeneous and foreign usurpation.

The coexistence of works such as the International Style Lovell houses on the one hand and the Californian Noble and Millikan houses on the other belied the contested historical ground they occupied. Like the political polemic, the architectural one between "us" and "them" reached a crescendo in the late 1920s and early '30s, but it had, in fact, begun much earlier and not within the California context. An attempt to define an appropriately American domesticity occurs, for example, in the writing of the architect Joy Wheeler Dow at the beginning of the century.[18] Rejecting the "newly-invented architecture" of the protomodernist, Midwestern Prairie School as undomestic, rootless, and foreign, Dow championed the revival of Georgian colonial architecture because its "Anglo-Saxon home feeling" suggested landed and familial continuity with the past. This attitude survived into the era between the wars. "The second onslaught of modernism upon America came not from the middle west," wrote Wells Bennett,[19] "but from abroad, [and that was] quite a different matter you may be sure. . . . Why, by this second and third decade of the twentieth century, doesn't everyone like modern architecture?" he asked. William Orr Ludlow's answer echoed Dow. He thought modern design suitable for commercial work, for skyscrapers, but "the sentiment about 'home' is not dead yet by any means. . . . The 'family' still means something, and as long

59

Fig. 46
George Howe (1886–1954),
William Stix Wasserman House,
Whitemarsh, Pennsylvania.

as it does the design of our homes is not going to be levelled to the utilitarian box. . . . Efficiency and iconoclasm will never wipe out that kind of sentiment that opposed to materialism makes life worth while."[20] Modernism remained undomestic, rootless, and foreign.

But the modernist had his viewpoint, too. In the words of George Howe, a man who had begun his career as a designer of regional works in eastern Pennsylvania and who was to codesign with European-born William Lescaze the first International Style skyscraper, the Philadelphia Savings Fund Society building (1929–32), "[I]n Modern Architecture . . . there is a greater beauty than in stylistic architecture; the beauty of the function and structural strength of character, instead of outward feature, based on true instead of false sentiment, and on the sound tradition of substance instead of the unsound tradition of form."[21] Howe might have had the Lovell and Noble houses in mind when he wrote elsewhere that "there is more real beauty in one straight line of a well-designed functional country house, standing in bold relief against the irregularities of nature, than in all the soft contours recreated by the romantic in painful imitation of the peasant's handiwork."[22] He was in an antiregionalist phase at that moment: "The functional architect," he wrote, "discarding all pretense at local character, rejoices in his freedom, and frankly brings together . . . materials from every quarter of the globe." But Howe, as an American architect between the wars, could not hold this internationalist position for long. When he wrote these words he was associated with the modernist Lescaze; later, on his own at the William Stix Wasserman House in Whitemarsh, Pennsylvania (fig. 46), he was to seek a compromise between modern forms and traditional local materials. In effect, he attempted to have it both ways, to establish a compromise position, to regionalize the International Style.[23]

But to return to California. Joy Wheeler Dow wrote for a WASP readership located largely in New England, where the English Colonial Revival had been one of the prevailing domestic architectural styles since the 1870s, but such "frigid, wood-begotten New England [architectural] types were poorly adapted, climatically and historically" to the South-

Fig. 47
Wilbur H. Collins House,
Pasadena, 1927.

Fig. 48
Collins House,
garden.

west, according to Newcomb, where each region was trying "to express itself in its own variant of this versatile sun-loving [Hispanic] style."[24] Wallace Neff, born and raised in California, studied art in Europe (the soft pencil drawings in his sketchbooks reflect an eye for picturesque rural buildings) and architecture in a program headed by a traditionalist and made at least one documented trip to Havana (late in 1924), where stuccoed walls, ceramic-tiled low-pitched roofs, and irregularly massed buildings sprouting corner chimneys caught his camera and pencil. He seems not to have written theory, permitting his Californian works to speak for his adherence to the prevailing Hispanic cultural definition of Southland regionalism. Neff's best works of the '20s adhere to an opposing line of architectural intention (figs. 47, 48), but whether or not he saw them as a polemical challenge to the works of Neutra or Schindler, and to what extent he thought of their work as rootless and foreign, is impossible to say. We suspect that he was too busy in that decade satisfying the requirements of exacting clients to worry about his place in architectural history. That would come later.[25]

The history of twentieth-century western architecture includes a range of works from traditionalist to modernist, but rare is the book that includes them all[26] and nonexistent the book that treats them with equal attention.[27] The polemical nature of modern historiography has led to a narrowly selective account of building in our century. That modernism, as a set of buildings and body of theory, is a constituent fact of the present century is indisputable. That it was but one constituent fact is also beyond question although rarely – until recently – admitted. That other buildings and ideas also existed, and in fact far outnumber the modern, has only become an acceptable observation in the postmodern era.[28]

That Neff and his like-minded colleagues turned out a distinguished body of work in the 1920s supported by a coherent theory of architectural regionalism can be overlooked only by the ideologue, the advocate, or the polemicist. Visits to the buildings of both camps provide a far more complete, richer picture of architecture between the wars than has existed in print.[29] California architecture of the 1920s and '30s includes distinguished work by both

Fig. 49
Bourne House.

sides – the California regionalism of Neff and the contemporary internationalism of Neutra (figs. 49, 50) – and no meaningful telling of the achievements of the era can neglect either one. Indeed, they are completely explicable only as a pair. Through exhibitions and in publications such as the present one, the unbalance of past histories is beginning to be redressed, and we are starting to view both the regional and the international styles – and their interrelationship – in a more accurate light.

Fig. 50
Richard Neutra,
Neutra House,
Los Angeles, 1933.

Notes

1. In this brief essay I can only suggest some aspects of this important topic, and I must sketch a simple picture in black and white that is, in fact, a far more complex pattern composed of subtle shades of gray.

2. Henry-Russell Hitchcock, Jr., and Philip Johnson, *The International Style: Architecture since 1922* (New York, 1932), p. 57. Elsewhere the authors modify the bluntness of this statement (p. 61) but permit only the architect "of courage" the use of curves, "with the sanctions of genius and in definite opposition to the discipline of regularity" (pp. 63–64).

   One review of the exhibition this book catalogues began its criticism of Le Corbusier's Villa Savoye with the comment: "[H]ere is a plan which binds itself absurdly into a system of supports" ("The Editor's Diary," *Architect* 65 [April 1932], p. 227).

3. Thomas S. Hines, *Richard Neutra and the Search for Modern Architecture* (New York and Oxford, 1982), p. 84 (and fig. 84).

4. Richard Neutra, *Life and Shape* (New York, 1962), pp. 221–222.

5. Remarks of the architect and the client make it sound as if a kind of regionalism operated in this design. Neutra found in Southern California as nowhere else at this date clients willing to build his work; Lovell is said to have observed that he was not going to build "my home the same as the woman from Peoria" (Hines [note 3], p. 78). The international elements of the design far outweigh casual and ambiguous remarks of this kind, however.

6. Hines (note 3), pp. 75–91, esp. 81; Neutra (note 4), p. 222; "The Demonstration Health-House," *Architectural Record* 67 (May 1930), pp. 433–438.

7. There is, as always, an exception to the generalization: the generous size of

the kitchen was apparently dictated by the demands of vegetarian cooking. Still, it was *shaped* by the frame. By 1962 Neutra had convinced himself that his goal had been *"To service with contemporary means organic life-needs"* [note 4], p. 224), but his discussion in *Life and Shape* of the design of the house begins with notes on technique (introduced with the revealing phrase "I had often thought . . ."), then proceeds to his client's vegetarian needs (pp. 222–224). That seems to re-create the process of design.

8. And according to the *Architectural Record* (note 6), the dimensions of the plan units of the frame were themselves determined by the size of the stock steel casement windows.

9. Hines (note 3), fig. 88.

10. Rexford Newcomb, *The Franciscan Mission Architecture of Alta California* (New York, 1916); *Mediterranean Domestic Architecture in the United States* (Cleveland, 1928); and *Spanish-Colonial Architecture in the United States* (New York, 1937); see also Ida M. Tarbell, *Florida Architecture of Addison Mizner* (New York, 1928). The periodicals of the '20s are peppered with articles on regional work in California and Florida.

11. It should be noted that Newcomb's region was flexible indeed. His book of 1928 includes examples from as far afield as Cleveland, Pittsburgh, and Wichita!

12. See Kevin Starr, *Inventing the Dream: California Through the Progressive Era* (New York and Oxford, 1985), *passim*.

13. David Gebhard, *Schindler* (New York, 1971), pp. 80–89; "A Beach House for Dr. P. Lovell at Newport Beach, California," *Architectural Record* 66 (September 1929), pp. 257–261.

14. *The New World Architecture* (London, New York, and Toronto, 1930), pp. 20–22, 260–272.

15. "The Spanish Colonial Revival in Southern California (1895–1930)," *Journal of the Society of Architectural Historians* 26 (May 1967), pp. 131–147.

16. *Mediterranean Domestic Architecture*, n.p. See especially the photographs of Neff's Bourne and Marion-Thomson houses in this volume. The photographer knew exactly what he was looking at. These characteristics appeared early in Neff's work. He is described as "a vivid realist who paints with strong shadows and bold form and rich color" by Harris Allen in "An Artist in Adobe," *Pacific Coast Architect* 26 (August 1924), p. 6.

17. "Personality in Regional Architecture: An Appreciation of the Work of Wallace Neff, Architect," *Western Architect* 35 (February 1926), p. 22.

18. *American Renaissance* (New York, 1904) (originally published in serial form in 1902); see esp. pp. 30–33.

19. "Modernism is Still in the Making," *Pencil Points* 12 (February 1931), pp. 87–88.

20. "Modernistic vs. Traditional Architecture," *Octagon* 2 (October 1930), pp. 10–11.

21. George Howe, "What is This Modern Architecture Trying to Express,"

American Architect 137 (May 1930), p. 108; see Robert A. M. Stern, *George Howe: Toward a Modern American Architecture* (New Haven and London, 1975). The Philadelphia Savings Fund Society building was included in Hitchcock and Johnson's catalogue (see note 2).

22. George Howe, "Functional Aesthetics and the Social Ideal," *Pencil Points* 13 (April 1932), pp. 215–218.

23. The original design was begun in partnership with Lescaze, but in 1932–34, on his own, Howe produced in Square Shadows, the Wasserman House, a work International Style in composition, modern in structure of reinforced concrete, but traditional in richly wrought, flexible spaces and textured, colorful walls of local stone and Virginia brick. The text of its initial publication (written by or with the help of the architect?) notes that in International Style work "it has seemed necessary to standardize methods of living to fit . . . [the] design." It also calls this "one more important contribution by an American architect to the history of world architecture." See "Square Shadows," *Architectural Forum* 62 (March 1935), pp. 192–205; see also Stern (note 21), pp. 163–166.

24. Newcomb, *Spanish-Colonial Architecture* (note 10), pp. 36–37. In fact, Californians in the early twentieth century built in every style from Spanish to modern, including the English Colonial: see, for example, Paul Robinson Hunter and Walter L. Reichardt, *Residential Architecture in Southern California* (n. pl., 1939), *passim*.

25. In fact too late. His own publication of his work, *Architecture of Southern California* (Chicago, 1964), is a name-dropping collection of mostly post–Second World War homes for Hollywood stars. It contains little that enhances his reputation.

26. Henry-Russell Hitchcock's *Architecture: Nineteenth and Twentieth Centuries* (Harmondsworth, Baltimore, and Victoria, 1958) is one that does. There is a chapter (24) entitled "Architecture Called Traditional in the Twentieth Century," but even in this book only 18 of 435 text pages are devoted to traditional work (and that does not include the Californian).

27. Recent histories, especially those written from other than stylistic points of view, have begun to produce more inclusive accounts. Among these are, for example, Leland M. Roth, *A Concise History of American Architecture* (New York, 1979), chap. 7: "Dichotomy: Tradition and the Avant Garde: 1915–1940," pp. 228ff.

28. Walter Kidney's *Architecture of Choice* (New York, 1974) errs on the other side by omitting any reference to modern design as an available option.

29. I mean, of course, in interpretative histories. In guidebooks such as David Gebhard and Robert Winter's *Architecture in Los Angeles and Southern California* (Salt Lake City, 1982), the works of both camps are admitted (although, in this edition at least, the Neutra entries far outnumber the Neffs).

An entirely new concept of

CONSTRUCTION

B U B B L E S

f o r

D E F E N S E

Jan Furey Muntz

The architecture of Southern California is unique in several ways. It is characterized by long, sweeping lines, flowing to conform with the surrounding terrain. Nowhere else is found such freedom in planning, gaiety in color, and beauty in conception. It is as if all the restrictions and shackles of the past had been lifted to let a new style emerge.[1]

That Wallace Neff believed in freedom of planning is nowhere more evident than in his designs for mass-produced housing. There was great interest in manufactured housing in the '30s and '40s. The original impetus was the Depression, which forced people out of their homes and removed the opportunity for young people to have a chance at the American dream of owning a single-family house. The Depression was followed by war, with bombs wiping out whole cities in Europe and the threat of the same happening in the United States. A whole new dimension was added to the housing problem. After World War II the Atomic Age brought even more anxiety about shelter and relocated cities.

With the mobilization of the entire country for World War II came shortages of any material used in warfare and the shift of the working force into concentrated geographic areas to support the defense industry. The sudden halt in private-sector development and luxury housing forced many architects to make rapid adjustments in their practices. Some worked for the military and government agencies; many did not survive the shift. Wallace Neff surveyed these changes with a global attitude. Although he was known as the architect to the stars, he was keenly aware of housing problems around the world and spent a great deal of time and effort on this problem. An inventor by nature, he came from a family of innovative thinkers. His grandfather, Andrew McNally, was the cartographer who founded Rand McNally and developed La Mirada and Altadena.[2] Since Neff grew up surrounded by men of vision who were developing Southern California, it is not surprising that he was aware of housing problems on an international scale.

Neff's first venture into mass-produced housing was the Honeymoon Cottage, a name coined by his most famous client, Mary Pickford. *American Home* claimed that it was America's first completely factory-built and portable house, a slight exaggeration.[3] *California Arts*

69

Previous Page
Fig. 51
**Advertisement illustration
for Airform Construction.**

Fig. 52
Honeymoon Cottage,
1934, installed on
Wilshire Boulevard.

Fig. 53
**Honeymoon Cottage
being moved by truck.**

and Architecture described it as "strikingly modern and distinctive" and published photographs in situ and completely furnished.[4] The cottage's virtues included the fact that it was engineered to withstand the stresses of earthquakes, storms, and truck transport. The carefully designed interior decor was white with doors, trim, and shutters in cobalt and light blue and what appear to have been Delft tiles surrounding the brick-lined fireplace. The structure was installed on Wilshire Boulevard in Los Angeles with a lighted sign displaying its name (fig. 52). The following year *American Architect* published the same photograph with another remarkable view of the house, precariously balanced on the flatbed of a truck, complete with tie-back ruffle curtains in the bay window (fig. 53).[5] Neff described this design as follows: "For some time I was possessed by the thought that there should be a demand for small homes of real charm within the reach of people of limited means. In brief, by application to small house construction of the same factory production methods that have at the same time so greatly reduced the cost and improved the quality of automobiles, we are now able to offer unique designs and features and careful attention to detail hitherto found only in homes costing a great deal more money."[6]

Construction was massive compared to present-day technology; the walls were six inches thick and entirely of redwood. Even the siding, ceilings, and roof were tongue and groove redwood. The brick chimney was steel reinforced and transported partially built. The living/dining room ceiling was panelled in knotty pine, but the rest of the redwood walls inside and out were painted white. There was a saving of four hundred dollars if one ordered the exterior stucco, interior plaster version. This obviously was not low-cost housing but rather small-scale custom housing.

In design, the massing of the Honeymoon Cottage was similar to Neff's large houses, including a formal front entrance with fanlight and louvered shutters. The shutters and tall chimney would reappear a few years later in a wildly different mass-produced house Neff designed. Always concerned with siting and natural light and heat, Neff provided shutters for the windows that were hinged at the top and swung up to provide awnings. The cottage had all

71

Fig. 54
Honeymoon Cottage,
living room and fireplace.

the elements of the archetypal house: a peaked roof, fireplace with wooden mantel and stately chimney (fig. 54), bay window, flowerpots, and shutters.[7]

Neff designed the Honeymoon Cottage when the development of mobile homes in the United States was gaining momentum. The cottage was only mobile to the extent that it could survive a trip from the factory to its foundation on a truck. Its dimensions are unknown, but it appears to have been much wider than the current single-width trailer. Neff talked about the advantage of having the services of an architect even though the house was very small. He pointed out that expensive detailing was possible due to mass production, yet the house would be delivered to its site within a few hours of the final color selection, just as in an automobile showroom. The caption in an *American Home* article in 1934 says it all: "When one of the country's finest architects designs a perfect little cottage that is portable, factory-built and incorporates A-1 materials, and costs $2,750 delivered to your lot – thats NEWS! But you need another bedroom? Pick up the telephone and order one – it will be sent out by the next truck and as quickly attached."[8]

Neff spent three years developing this idea and evidently invested quite a bit of his own money in the project.[9] He even incorporated a provision for expansion by designing two shelves on a blank exterior wall to hold pots of flowers until the additional room was ordered and attached. As an added incentive for young buyers, special monthly financing could be arranged. An interesting alliance was formed to produce the house; the interiors were designed by Barker Brothers, Inc., a large Los Angeles interior design firm. A variety of designs, from one to five bedrooms, was offered, but there is no evidence that these alternatives were ever carried out.

By 1936 there were four hundred manufacturers producing forty thousand house trailers a year in the United States, and the industry was purported to be the fastest-growing one in the country, responding to the displaced people of the Depression.[10] Historically, this industry has been entered successfully by people who did not come from the traditional

Fig. 56
Bubble House,
Falls Church, Virginia, 1941.

building industry, people who were not hampered by traditional methods and materials. Wallace Neff certainly is a classic example of this, building six-inch walls and wood-paneled houses with bay windows and tall chimneys. He essentially translated a luxury home to a mini scale. This did not guarantee success in the industry, however. Although many people were living in trailer homes at the time, the Honeymoon Cottage was not a success. In 1977, for instance, the average price of a factory-built mobile home was $8.95 per square foot. The cost of the cottage was approximately $5.50 per square foot in 1934, definitely not low-cost housing. But Neff had vision and learned from his experience with the Honeymoon Cottage. In 1941, just a few years after his venture into mass-produced mobile housing, he abandoned traditional construction methods and vocabulary and produced his first Bubble House or Airform Construction.

The impetus for this type of construction was the intense need to provide economical fire- and bomb-resistant housing for defense workers and war-evacuated populations. Neff's first project was in Falls Church, Virginia, where twelve experimental houses were built for defense workers (figs. 55, 56). These first shells were twenty-three feet in diameter, single shells and double insulated shells in several combinations and configurations, primarily hemispheres with the exception of one barrel vault. It was found that the single shell was not suitable for the Virginia climate due to sweating, but the double shells were judged comfortable and energy efficient. *Life* described the new colony as "a mushroom village of odd little white houses [that] has sprouted in recent weeks."[11] The houses had organic forms and were somewhat startling, especially in the grove of tall trees where they were constructed on Horseshoe Hill in Fairfax County. The actual design of these houses, identical to Neff's patent application of 1941,[12] is primitive in plan and fenestration. There is a photograph in the *Life* article of a small clay model on which Neff had hand-painted landscaping and shutters. He paid homage to the colonial setting by making the shutters dark and laying hardwood floors over the concrete slab. The opening of these houses caused traffic jams; over five thousand Washingtonians came to see them.

75

Fig. 57
**Wallace Neff and
Mexican dignitaries in front of an
Airform Construction project.**

This first Bubble House commission came through a client, King Vidor, and his association with Jesse Jones, then director of Defense Homes Corporation, an agency that provided equity investments for rental projects. The bubbles cost less than three thousand dollars each at the time and used only fifteen pounds of nails, which Neff claims could have been eliminated. The reaction to these strange forms was not always positive. *Architectural Forum* observed:

> *Similarly shaped houses have been designed by Harvard's Professor Martin Wagner and Inventor Buckminster Fuller with the Butler Manufacturing Company, and have been lived in for years by the Eskimos. . . . At month's end opinions of the balloon or bubble house were in conflict; the Army was said to be interested in the construction system for building concrete balloon "tents," airplane hangars and powder magazines; some reporters predicted it to be the house of the future; some observers considered it unfortunate that public funds were being spent on such a spectacularly unorthodox house; and some predicted that Architect Neff's ideas would burst long before his bubble.* [13]

In the same year that the Bubble Houses were built in Virginia and published, Buckminster Fuller was indeed converting Butler grain storage bins into houses. These looked remarkably like grain storage bins with portholes in spite of their elegant name, "Dymaxion Deployment Unit." [14] Professor Wagner at Harvard was creating colonies of metal teepees that had attributes similar to the Bubble House but that were more industrial in appearance. The unique aspects of Neff's approach were the lack of formal and material constraint and his fascination with designing within these parameters. These houses underscore his demonstrated skill in understanding a design vocabulary and utilizing it rather than applying it in a superficial manner.

The published material of the 1930s and '40s indicates much experimentation in mass-produced housing in concrete, yet it was always within the form of rectilinear wood-

frame construction. One of many such published houses was a design by the notable architect Paul Williams published in *California Arts and Architecture*. Although the house used preformed concrete panels, its form was conventional both in plan and elevation.[15] Neff's design looks radical today, but even at the time he predated Fuller's experiments with geodesic domes and the Italians' development of thin shell concrete design. Since his dome houses were published around the world in both technical journals and popular magazines, there is no doubt that his work was seminal in the development of thin shell construction.

The idea of using a bubble form for concrete was not original to Neff; what was original was the development and refinement of the process, the search for technical solutions, the application of the project to contemporary housing problems, and the pleasure of designing within a circular form – something he obviously enjoyed, utilizing it frequently in his work.[16] Neff refers in his notes to an article in *Architect and Engineer* published in 1933 that influenced his own thinking. In it Norman W. Mohr, an architect from San Francisco, explains his idea, evidently patented in 1920, for "A new Style of Architecture by a New type of Construction." Mohr had been inspired by another article, published in 1927, describing construction with an inflatable form. He was fascinated not only by the speed and economy of construction but also, like Neff, with the design possibilities of the curve generated by the balloon form. Mohr describes the beauty and advantages of the circular form such as strength, sanitation, acoustics, and resistance to horizontal stress, which he calls "air inventions."[17] This list is similar to Neff's list of the advantages of Airform Construction:

1. *The buildings are permanently Class "A" structures.*

2. *Fire, earthquake and storm resistant.*

3. *Bomb, concussion and splinter resistant.*

4. *Vermin and termite proof.*

5. *Economy of construction.*

6. Low upkeep costs.

7. Saving on fuel for heating.

8. Cool in summer.

9. Non-critical materials in abundance almost everywhere.

10. Ease and speed in construction.[18]

Neff was inspired by the chambered nautilus and derived from nature the elliptical shape into which the Bubble House eventually evolved. Not so with his later collaborator, Eliot Noyes, who claimed to have improved the appearance of the Bubble Houses[19] but who ignored the circular form and superimposed a rectangle. It is interesting to note that he also opened up the bottom of the dome, thereby giving up all of its inherent stability and strength.[20] An illustrated model for Noyes's house is an absolute rectangle and does not even show the Airform structure of the roof.[21] He did not use the inherent plastic quality of thin shell concrete, trying to make it conform to conventional wood frame construction. Neff, on the other hand, exulted in the forms and even made the point that partitions should not go to the ceiling, so that the curve would be visible and part of the space.[22] Not only was this low-cost housing; it was unique and created beautiful interior spaces. Where else could one find similar housing with twelve-foot ceilings?

The Bubble Houses frequently were referred to as igloos; Neff preferred, later, to use the name Airform Construction.[23] The construction method was as important to him as the design. His work, combining material and method with design, ranks him with the modern masters, such as Konrad Wachsmann and Walter Gropius, who developed the General Panel Houses for mass housing at the same time that Neff was developing the Bubble House. Wachsmann felt that the material of construction was equally as important as the design and had a direct relationship to it.[24]

The early 1940s marked the apex of research and development in mass-produced

Fig. 60
**Balloon being removed through
Bubble House window after initial
shell had set.**

Fig. 61
**Anchoring a Bubble House balloon to
the catenary ring.**

Fig. 62
**Completed Bubble House dome with
wire mesh tied around the outside.**

housing. *Architectural Forum* ran a monthly article on building for defense, tracking contracts and design development and reporting that "bureaucracy, traditions and labor unions steer prefabrication past proving grounds to burial grounds." It predicted accurately the ultimate fate of mass use of prefabricated housing.[25] When the need for mass housing ended with the war, Neff pursued foreign development and built villages in Brazil, Pakistan, western Africa, Mexico (fig. 57), Jordan, and the Virgin Islands. He also developed alternative uses for the Airform, including a dome farm for wine storage in Portugal (fig. 58) and grain storage bins in Arizona. He was comfortable with the technology of architecture, partly due to his studies at MIT, and shared his office building in Pasadena with the innovative engineer Fritz Ruppel, inventor of the Latisteel concrete and steel frame building system.[26] Neff spent a great deal of time researching forms and concrete; in fact, much of the archival material left today consists of letters to manufacturers looking not only for an inflatable form that would work but also for one that would be cost effective. Neff went to great lengths to describe the point that his mass-produced buildings were not constructed in the usual sense, which he related to the root of the word *construct*, "to pile on." "Beautiful flowing lines and curves come into being without effort. . . . The absolute absence of girders, columns, and jigsaw trusses, startles the imagination," he wrote. Neff related the form of the Airform to the form of the earth: "Airform buildings deflect the sun's heat waves, much as the earth does in polar regions."[27]

      Airform Construction was unique in that it used a double insulated dome. The first shell poured over the Airform would actually become the form for the second shell (fig. 59). Once the initial shell had set, the balloon was removed through a door or window and construction on another dome could begin (fig. 60). It was estimated that one hundred domes could be built in sixty days or two hundred in ninety days using only four balloon forms in the construction process. Another remarkable feature was that the construction was weather protected in twenty-four hours, since roof, walls, and exterior finish were one and the same. The continuous thrust at the base of the dome had to be resisted to stabilize the

83

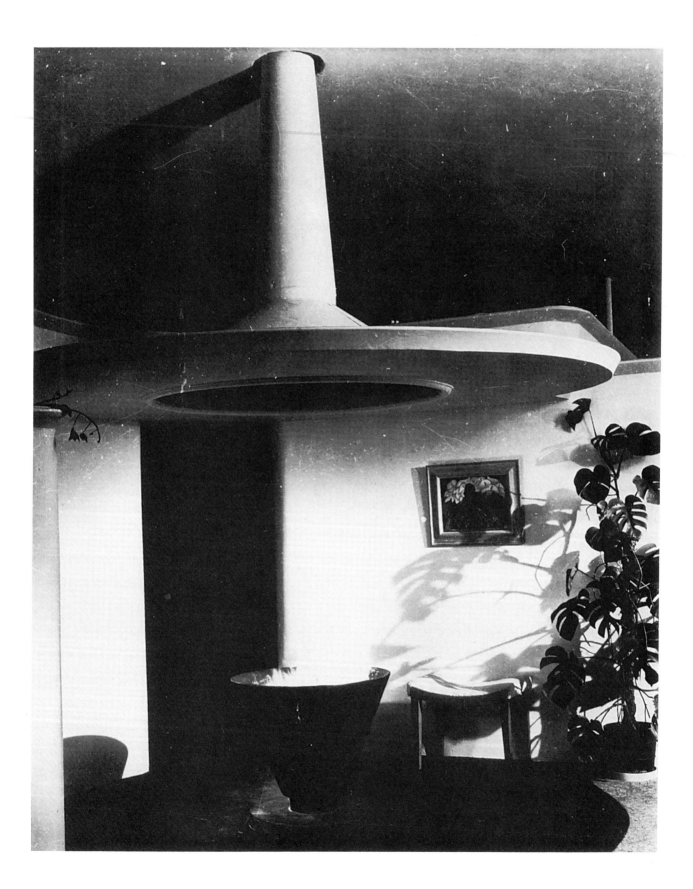

Fig. 63
**Interior of Bubble House with
freestanding fireplace.**

form. Neff took care of this with a catenary ring, which also anchored the inflated Airform (fig. 61). Openings disrupted structural continuity and presented the most difficult design problem to resolve. Neff prized the design's natural ability to deflect bomb fragments and radiation, a cause of national concern when he was designing the Bubble Houses. He took advantage of the natural transfer of forces in a dome – compression on the top, tension on the bottom – and deformed the structure by the weight of Gunite applied from the top and raised the vertical wall by tying wire mesh around the outside (fig. 62). Neff felt that his dome could be built by native labor in developing countries and that the concrete shell might be applied by hand.

Neff was intrigued by the fact that such a small amount of air pressure could support this inflatable form. He continued to experiment and refine the technique and discovered that reducing air pressure from 1½ psi to ¾ psi allowed the ceiling height to drop; more height was then gained at the side walls. The first homes had straight side walls to only four feet, but this was gradually increased to close to six feet, allowing for a more functional space. Professor George Hausner of California Institute of Technology, an internationally known seismic expert, remembers Neff consulting with him on improving the structure of the domes even more in the early '60s.[28]

Neff initially chose Goodyear Rubber Company to produce the inflatable form. This eventually led to the construction of a desert colony in Litchfield Park, Arizona, a town owned and planned by Goodyear. These houses, published in *Architectural Record*,[29] appear to fit in well with the landscape. They were furnished in a traditional style that seems to have worked within the dome. Most interesting is the fact that the interior view with the fireplace mantel and drapes and sheers at the windows (fig. 63) gives no clue to the startling appearance of this colony of domes. Garages and pergolas were added to the exteriors. The classical columns supporting the pergolas were actually clay sewer pipes filled with concrete and stuccoed on the exterior. The plan used a double dome with the space between utilized for entry, kitchen, and bath. This connecting space evolved into a solarium or living room, allowing three bedrooms in the double dome plan

Fig. 64
Floor plan, elevations, and construction details for a Type "E" Bubble House,
Litchfield Park, Arizona.

Fig. 65
Manuel Reachi House Project,
Ensenada, Mexico, 1954.

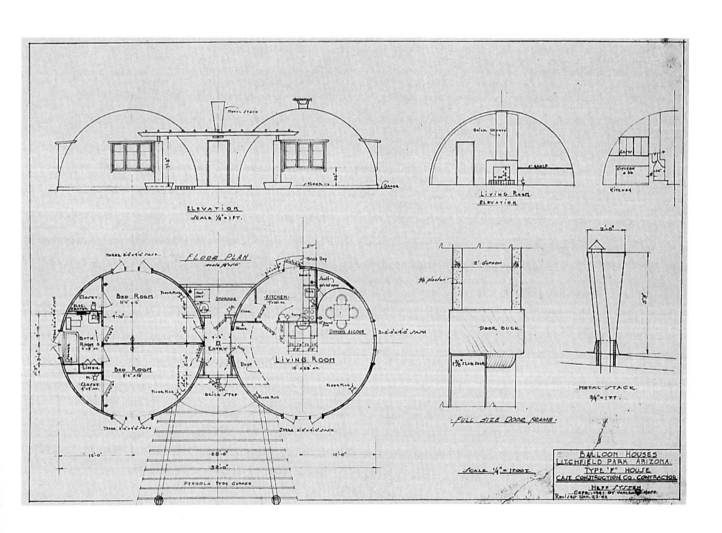

(fig. 64).[30] Neff also built a number of domes for grain storage in the same town.

The architecturally most exciting design incorporating the Airform was a house for the movie director Manuel Reachi in Mexico. Unfortunately, the house was never built, but it was the most successful integration of the thin shell dome into a conventional luxury home, utilizing a Beaux-Arts plan. Only the plan and an evocative rendering survive (fig. 65).[31]

The true test of a structure like the Bubble House is an evaluation by another architect. In 1969 Virginia Tanzmann, AIA, drove by one on Alta Vista Drive in South Pasadena and was attracted to it immediately. The owner, Mrs. Wallace Neff, had grown too ill to negotiate the stairs to the house. Tanzmann subsequently bought the house, about which she has stated emphatically: "It was wonderful!" The space functioned beautifully, and an eclectic collection of furniture fit comfortably into the elliptical plan. Tanzmann recalls the annual search to find a twelve-foot-high Christmas tree for the living room. She feels that the house was sited perfectly, taking advantage of the natural light and views. As an architect, she still marvels at the efficiency of the plan and can only remember having trouble with the wall curvature in one isolated "corner" of the kitchen. Tanzmann never met Wallace Neff, but within hours of the Sylmar earthquake in 1971 he called to ask about the condition of the house.[32]

The stability of the Bubble House dome was an important element to Neff, and he wrote about it a great deal. A memorable photograph shows someone whacking the side of a Bubble House with an axe (fig. 66). The Pasadena Building Department was skeptical about the strength of the thin shell and required Neff to build and load to failure the concrete dome. As usual, the well-connected Neff brought in a professor from Caltech to engineer the testing.
He was proud of the fact that the dome held the load.

In *House Out of Factory*, a survey of factory-made housing published in 1946, the Bubble House is the first one illustrated and the only house in the whole book with a curved plan (not including the Fuller grain bin, which was not designed but rather taken off the

87

Fig. 66
**Hitting a Bubble House dome
with an axe,**
1940s.

shelf).[33] Although one of the book's authors relegated the "Bubble Houses in an American Village" to a chapter entitled "Modernism and the Inhumanists,"[34] forty-eight years later Neff's idea still has merit. As Alson Clark has stated, "[Neff's] supreme invention, one which qualified him for status as a modern pioneer, was the Bubble House or Airform Structure of 1941."[35]

At the end of his life Neff lived in the Bubble House in Pasadena that he had built for his brother (fig. 67) and never gave up his dreams for this design. It appears that this house is the only extant Airform Construction in the United States, the Arizona and Virginia complexes having been destroyed for higher density land development, the South Pasadena house a casualty of the Whittier earthquake. Neff's description of the construction method for the Airform (fig. 68) goes into great technical detail and would enable anyone to build from his set of specifications. All the knowledge gained over thirty-five years of research and development is contained in the document, including a detailed cost estimate.[36] Much of the information is given as if a professor were training a student to think about the process. ". . . Now let's figure the weight. Referring to page 42 a 60$'$ sphere has a surface area of 5,655 sq. ft.," Neff noted, launching into detailed calculations to determine the weight. He was eighty-one years old when he wrote the method's final version.

According to Nikolaus Pevsner, "the Modern Movement in architecture, in order to be fully expressive of the twentieth century, had to possess both qualities, the faith in science and technology, in social and rational planning, and the romantic faith in speed and the roar of machines."[37] Neff not only made a major modernist statement but also was able to resolve the dilemma of being an architect close to affluent clients and a designer for a mass of anonymous clients with low budgets. He earned his place in architectural history.

Fig. 67
Dr. Andrew Neff Bubble House,
Pasadena, 1946.

This chronological list was discovered in Wallace Neff's personal papers. It was compiled by Neff, typewritten until 1954, then handwritten. A few additions have been made by this author. It is interesting to see the continuing interest in a building type that was essentially abandoned in the United States after World War II and Wallace Neff's personal lifelong dedication to the project.

  A search made to determine the status of the Bubble Houses in the United States indicated that all of the known American projects have been demolished, the one exception being the house in Pasadena that Neff built for his brother.

Los Angeles Times
1941.

March of Time Radio News
November 27, 1941.

Architectural Forum 75
December 1941, p. 421.

Architectural Record 90
December 1941, pp. 22, 108.

Life
December 1, 1941, pp. 24–25.

Michigan Society of Architects 18
1942, pp. 4–5.

Portland Cement Association
1942, p. CP 50.

Architect and Engineer 148
January 1942, pp. 20–23.

Catholic Digest
January 1942, pp. 80–81.

National Real Estate Journal
January 1942.

Newsweek
January 1942.

Western Construction News
January 1942, p. 12.

Time
January 5, 1942, pp. 36–37.

Illustrated London News
January 10, 1942.

The Architect's Journal 95
January 22, 1942, pp. 72–74.

Sie und Er
February 6, 1942.

The United States News
February 13, 1942.

Concrete Builder
Spring 1942, pp. 8–9.

Fortune
March 1942, p. 155.

Popular Mechanics
March 1942, p. 7.

Hollands – Magazine of The South
April 1942.

Nuestra Arquitectura 14
May 1942, pp. 174–177.

Arizona Farmer
July 18, 1942, p. 3.

Christian Science Monitor
July 31, 1942.

Christian Science Monitor
September 2, 1942.

Christian Science Monitor
September 14, 1942.

The Book of Knowledge
1943, pp. 178–181.

Architectural Forum 178
February 1943, pp. 76–78.

Architect & Building News 174
April 23, 1943, p. 60.

Engineering News Record 131
December 2, 1943, p. 55.

Engineering News Record 131
December 16, 1943, p. 69.

Forbes
January 1944.

The Indiana Farmers Guide
January 1944.

Southwest Builder & Contractor
February 11, 1944, cover.

Engineering News Record 132
February 24, 1944, p. 97.

The Goodall News
March 1944.

Forbes
April 1944.

Fortune
May 1944, p. 170.

Popular Mechanics 81
May 1944, pp. 45–48.

Architectural Record 96
July 1944, pp. 81–83.

Country Gentleman
July 1944.

Southwest Builder & Contractor
July 28, 1944.

Engineering News Record 133
August 10, 1944, p. 77.

Engineering News Record 133
November 18, 1944.

Pacific Rural Press
December 25, 1944.

John B. Pierce Foundation
1945.

Prefabrication
September 4, 1945, pp. 38–40.

Liberty
September 29, 1945, p. 30.

Goodyear Triangle 37
November 20, 1945.

Popular Mechanics
January 1946.

Picture Wise
May 1946, p. 22.

See
September 1946, p. 24.

Los Angeles Home Magazine
April 13, 1947.

Revista de la Esquela National de
Arquitectura 22
June 1947, pp. 58–61.

West Coast Real Estate & Business
Opportunity Journal
June 1947, p. 10.

Architectural Forum 87
July 1947, p. 15.

A Rodovia
November 1947, p. 54.

Manama
December 13, 1947.

Plastering Industries
January 1948, pp. 14–15.

Engineering News Record 140
April 22, 1948, p. 5.

Engineering News Record
1949, p. 34.

Rubber 1
February 5, 1949, p. 15.

Engineering News Record
August 25, 1949, p. 5.

Fortune
October 1949, p. 14.

Goodyear "Junior"
1950.

Housing – MIT
1950.

Journal of the American Institute of
Architects 14
November 1950, p. 221.

Christian Science Monitor
November 10, 1950, p. 10.

Interiors
March 1951, p. 14.

Engineering News Record
June 1951, p. 55.

The Constructor
1953.

Epoca
1953, pp. 31–33.

Reader's Digest
June 1953, pp. 98–99.

Time
June 22, 1953, p. 62.

Prefabrication
November 1953, p. 22.

Popular Science
December 1953, pp. 133–135.

Engineering News Record
December 24, 1953, p. 45.

Mademoiselle
January 1954, p. 91.

Vogue
January 1954, p. 127.

Christian Science Monitor
January 15, 1954, p. 10.

Time
January 25, 1954, p. 104.

Life
February 22, 1954, pp. 75–78.

House & Home
March 1954, p. 153.

American Industrial Exporter Special
Report
May 1954, pp. 51–58.

Architectural Record
May 1954, pp. 314, 316.

Progressive Architecture 35
June 1954, pp. 116–119.

Architectural Record
November 1954, pp. 221, 223.

House & Home
January 1955, p. 134.

Architectural Record
February 1955, pp. 206–208.

Business Week
January 5, 1957.

Time
August 18, 1959, pp. 24–26.

Junior Scholastic 47
January 25, 1961, p. 8.

Shell Architecture
1963.

United Nations Review 2
March 1964, cover.

Los Angeles Times
June 10, 1982.

Pasadena Star News
June 10, 1982.

Pasadena Star News
May 17, 1987, p. B-1.

Pasadena Star News
May 11, 1989, p. B-1.

Notes

1. Wallace Neff, Architect, FAIA, *Architecture of Southern California* (Chicago, 1964), Foreword.

2. Andrew McNally selected the name *Altadena* for the new town and proposed the name *Bajadena* for what was to become South Pasadena. See Margaret Stoval, "Arthur Libby Neff's Roots Planted Deeply in Pasadena," *Pasadena Star-News*, October 9, 1971.

3. Warwick Carpenter, "Cottage for Two," *American Home* 12 (November 1934), pp. 366, 377, 424.

4. "Honeymoon Cottage," *California Arts and Architecture* 46 (August 1934), p. 23.

5. "Honeymoon Cottage," *American Architect* 146/2631 (March 1935), p. 72.

6. Statement by Wallace Neff in Carpenter (note 3).

7. Charles W. Moore, Kathryn Smith, and Peter Becker, *Home Sweet Home — American Domestic Vernacular Architecture* (New York, 1983), pp. 98–117.

8. See above (note 3).

9. Wallace Neff, Jr., ed., and Alson Clark, *Wallace Neff: Architect of California's Golden Age* (Santa Barbara, 1986), p. 127.

10. Arthur D. Bernhardt, *Building Tomorrow: The Mobile/Manufactured Housing Industry* (Boston, 1980), p. 29.

11. "Balloon Houses Designed For Defense Workers Bloom Under Virginia Trees," *Life* (December 1, 1941), pp. 34–35.

12. Patent Application 1941, Wallace Neff Papers, Huntington Library and Art Gallery, San Marino.

13. "Building for Defense: Ballyhooed Balloon," *Architectural Forum* 75 (December 1941), p. 421.

14. "Building for Defense – 1,000 Houses a Day at $1,200 Each," *Architectural Forum* 69 (June 1941), pp. 425–429.

15. Paul R. Williams, Architect, "A Prefabricated Model Home," *California Arts and Architecture* (January 1939).

16. Neff's fascination with the circle began early in his career and was first expressed in the circular Fred Niblo House in Beverly Hills in 1926, followed by the Sidney L. Berg House in Pasadena in 1927. These houses form circular voids in the center which could have been the beginning of the bubble houses. See Neff, Jr., and Clark (note 9).

17. "Thumb Tacks and T-Square," *Architect and Engineer* (August 1933), p. 4.

18. Wallace Neff, AIA, "Airform Construction," September 1949, Wallace Neff Papers, Huntington Library and Art Gallery, San Marino.

19. "Airformed Concrete Domes," *Progressive Architecture* (June 1954), pp. 116–119.

20. "Semitropical Igloo," *Life* (February 22, 1954), pp. 75–76.

21. "A Bubble of Ballooned Concrete Forms a Radically New Kind of House," *Architectural Record Houses of 1956* (May 1956), pp. 204–205.

22. Wallace Neff, Architect, FAIA, *Thin Shell Concrete Construction (Airform)*, June 1976, p. 13, Wallace Neff Papers, Huntington Library and Art Gallery, San Marino.

23. An igloo is built by piling ice bricks in a continuous spiral, with only the vault for the door breaking the dome's surface, while Neff pointed out that his method of construction did not use the conventional piling on of material.

24. See Esther McCoy, "Konrad Wachsmann Obituary," *L.A. Architect* 7 (January 1981), p. 3.

25. "Building for Defense," *Architectural Forum* 73 (March 1941), pp. 3, 174.

26. "Latisteel Concrete Wall Panels," *Architectural Forum* 85 (July 1946), p. 113.

27. See above (note 21).

28. Interview with the author.

29. "Airform house for a desert Colony," *Architectural Record* 96 (July 1944), p. 83.

30. Construction drawings, Wallace Neff Papers, June 1942, Huntington Library and Art Gallery, San Marino.

31. Neff, Jr., and Clark (note 9), p. 208.

32. Interview with the author.

33. John Gloag, ARIBA, and Grey Wornum, FRIBA, *House Out of Factory* (London, 1946), pp. 17–19.

34. John Gloag, *Men and Buildings* (London, 1950), p. 233.

35. Neff, Jr., and Clark (note 9), p. 28.

Fig. 68
**Mrs. Thomas Ince
Bubble House
under construction,**
South Pasadena, 1946.

36. The document was reviewed by Marion Zuro, a Los Angeles concrete contractor, for its relevance to today's concrete industry. Mr. Zuro was impressed by the innovative methods for the time but felt that the labor costs today would be prohibitive for mass housing in the United States.

37. Nikolaus Pevsner, *Pioneers of Modern Design from William Morris to Walter Gropius* (New York, 1960), p. 210.

BUILDING, DRAWING, THINKING:

WALLACE NEFF and the PRACTICE

of AMERICAN ECLECTICISM

in the 1920s

Stefanos Polyzoides
and Charles Calvo

Wallace Neff was a distinguished architect who, in the 1920s, produced some of the most remarkable eclectic houses of California's golden age. This architecture speaks eloquently about social institutions, building craft, and design visions, and its power is the result of a hierarchical, collaborative building process, at the heart of which lay a broadly held, carefully structured understanding about drawing.

The common view holds that it was the decline of craftsmanship that caused the collapse of eclecticism after 1930. Yet, it is evident from an examination of Wallace Neff's drawings that this explanation is inadequate. It is the premise of this essay that this collapse was due to the weakening of the links among thinking, drawing, and building in the process of making architecture.

All great architecture has at its source the effective collaboration of three parties: the client, the architect, and the builder. Clients in the 1920s demanded houses that evoked the origins of western civilization in America. In California the source of culture was most often sought in the construction traditions of the Mediterranean (figs. 69, 70). Both vernacular and classical precedents were used according to the circumstances. These precedents were recorded, transformed, and made available through the common language of drawing. In this period architectural drawing, or draughting, comprised several drawing forms: the travel sketch, the presentation drawing, and the working drawing. Such was the consistency of attitude regarding the recording and transmission of architectural images and ideas that even the photograph, the final step in the documentation process, may be included in the discussion.

Draughtsmanship

Draughting, in the early part of the twentieth century in the United States, was understood as a clearly defined subdivision of the architectural profession. Indeed, the discipline even warranted its own magazine, *Pencil Points*, which covered issues ranging from

Fig. 71
**Hugh Ferriss, drawing illustrated on
the cover of *Pencil Points*,**
1925.

sketching to technical news and construction techniques (fig. 71). Draughtsmen were well known and often circulated among the offices of early Southern California architects as the demands of various projects waxed and waned.[1] These professionals played a critical role in the execution of buildings, taking the ideas of the architect and developing them in a form that could be constructed. The discipline required strong drawing skills, technical knowledge, and an understanding of design rather than design talent itself.

The origins of architectural draughtsmanship as a profession may be traced to the Renaissance, when the architect as artist and intellectual was distinguished from the medieval architect as master builder. The rise of organized architectural education promoted the tradition of the architect as the originator of design ideas and established the profession of architecture as distinguished and worthy of respect. In the United States in the nineteenth century, manual arts colleges rose apace with the architecture schools being established at major universities. These colleges gave the student a greater knowledge of trades than is part of the general architectural curriculum today. This second pedagogy established the role of the draughtsman as a technical adjunct to that of the architect. The apprencticeship system also reinforced the role of draughtsmanship, as apprentices learned their trade by tracing the drawings of the master architect or draughtsman.

The necessity for good draughtsmanship arose from many factors. Primary among these was the variety of architectural orders embraced by historic eclecticism and the wealth of new building materials and assemblies ushered in by the Industrial Revolution. By the opening of the twentieth century the practice of architecture required both a sophisticated visual vocabulary – encompassing a range of architectural forms and styles – and an equally sophisticated technical vocabulary – providing the means by which to execute the forms. Both of these
required a powerful means of communication. While all three principals in the architectural
process approached architecture differently, all shared its visual and experiential aspects
Drawings therefore had to convey experiential information so the client could envision and

GRUYÈRES
OCT 19 1914

100

Fig. 72
Street View Perspective,
Gruyères[?], France,
1914.

evaluate the work and the builder could envision and construct it. As any language grows more sophisticated when the thoughts it is required to express grow more sophisticated, so draughtmanship at the turn of the century grew as the demands of the profession expanded.

The draughtsmanship of the early twentieth century may best be distinguished from that of our own by its insistence on a vision of a whole predicated on experience. From sketch through presentation drawing to working drawing and photograph, the viewer could get a sense of the whole work depicted; that whole was not confined to form alone but included issues of light, material, texture, and so on.

Sketches

The means of transferring architectural ideas from historical examples to current applications in the early part of this century were the travel sketch (fig. 72), the measured detail, and the travel photograph. The culture of architecture was shared so pervasively that details, sketches, and photographs were widely used independent of the particular derivations or precedents of individual examples. In fact, the communality of attitude regarding the recording of architectural ideas from extant work was so focused that it resulted in a common vocabulary for drawing. It is difficult at best to identify the sketches or measured drawings of one architect of this period from those of another.

From the Renaissance onward architectural sketches served two purposes. They were a means of recording what was seen for future reference, and they were a means of expressing architectural ideas for future development. In both cases the sketch is evidence of a way of seeing, recording aspects seen or envisioned that are of greatest importance to the person sketching. The personal collections of travel documents of the architects of this period were evidence of the breadth of their visual education and the authenticity of their intentions. Inherent in these sketches were the sources of important future buildings and the claim to a leading role in professional practice.

Fig. 73
Fred Niblo House
Beverly Hills, 1926,
sections and plot plan, detail,
drawn by Arthur E. Fisk.

Fig. 74
Niblo House,
first floor plan,
drawn by W. De H.

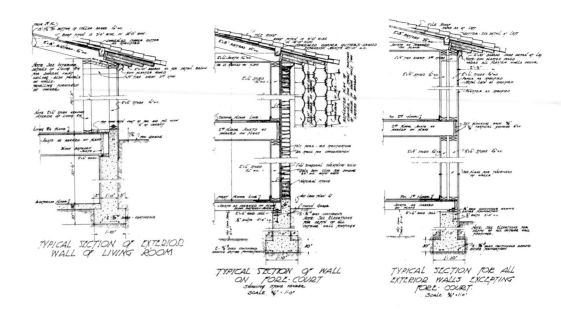

TYPICAL SECTION OF EXTERIOR
WALL OF LIVING ROOM

TYPICAL SECTION OF WALL
ON FORE-COURT
SHOWING STOVE FENDER
SCALE ¾" = 1'-0"

TYPICAL SECTION FOR ALL
EXTERIOR WALLS EXCEPTING
FORE-COURT
SCALE ¾" = 1'-0"

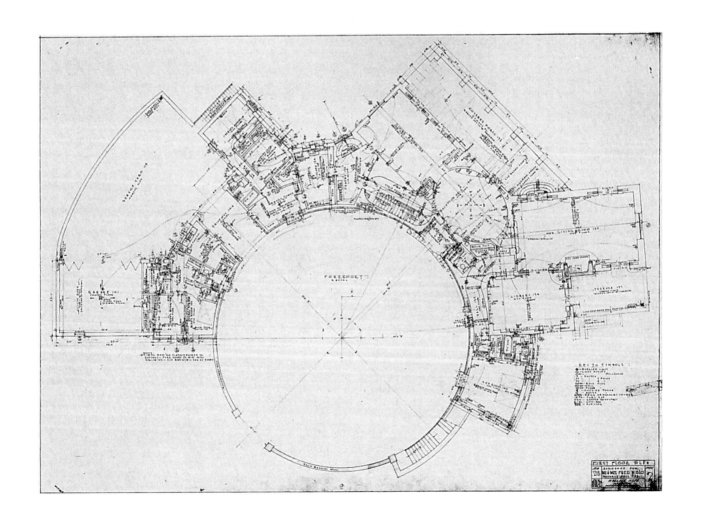

Fig. 75
**Averell Harriman
Ski Lodge Project,**
*Sun Valley, Idaho, 1940,
rendering by Carl Oscar Borg.*

Presentation Drawings

Architectural patrons in the first part of this century demanded that building design be based on references to genuine historic visual fragments. These demands were on occasion taken to extremes, as in the case of James Waldron Gillespie, who took his architect, Bertram Goodhue, to India and Persia in 1902 to establish a common vocabulary for the design of his house and gardens. Even without such enlightened patronage, architects were well prepared to extend their experiences with historical precedents into new compositions.

The principal tools for the generation of architectural form in the 1920s were the sketch plan and the perspective. Although such drawings seem to be very general and often picturesque, they tend to establish conclusively the salient qualities of the object in question. It was not uncommon for even modest presentation drawings eloquently to evoke architecture, landscape, and urban character, since eclectic architects were capable of conceiving their work on many scales simultaneously. In terms of building materials and systems, however, presentation drawings were vague. In the end, all eclectic work emphasized theatrical effect, and therefore issues of "making" were purposely left elusive (fig. 75). The absence of specific instructions in the drawings allowed the builder to participate actively in the building process by contributing his expertise in matters of construction.

Working Drawings

While construction technology in the early decades of the twentieth century was rapidly increasing in complexity, the tradition of draughtsmanship continued to demand that construction and construction documents be thought of as prescriptive of a high level of craftsmanship (figs. 73, 74). The working drawings of this period should be understood not as a set of specific instructions but as a comprehensive set of design intentions for construction. The

Fig. 76
Edward L. Doheny
Memorial Library,
Saint John's Seminary,
Camarillo, 1939.

builder/contractor was seen as a partner in the building process whose role was to realize the experiences depicted in the drawings. Thus, the latter tend to indicate in explicit ways the intended final experience of building space, form, and finish, while they are vague at best about the details of construction. The contractor was given only the information that was essential to the visual and experiential intentions of the architect and the requirements of structural or constructive integrity. The builder was then to execute these intentions in the best traditions of his craft.

Further evidence of this attitude may be found in the beauty of the working drawings of this period. Whether from such offices as those of Cram, Goodhue, and Ferguson or from the smaller offices of residential architects such as those of Southern California, these drawings are as carefully crafted and meticulously executed as the buildings they depicted were intended to be. The builder working with such a set could not fail to appreciate the architect's attention to detail, finish, and integrity.

Photography

Photographs of buildings produced within the eclectic tradition represent the same attitudes as the drawings that generated those buildings. These images range from overall views of the buildings in context to details, places, or moments within the edifices themselves (figs. 76–78). They attempt to capture the sense of integrity found in the drawings. This quality should not be confused with a sense of entirety. Rather than exhaustively portraying the building with endless images, the architect and photographer chose and structured each image so that it might represent the *idea* of the building as a whole.

The training of architects and draughtsmen at the turn of the century was based on a specific way of seeing, drawing, and making the world. It generated overlapping but distinctly different professional roles within a shared vision of architectural form. This vision was also easily understood by both client and builder. It meant that while each player in the architectural process could and did think about the building quite differently, all could see it

and discuss it through a common drawing vocabulary. With such a powerful tool, it is not surprising that extraordinary buildings were created. It is also not surprising that as belief in the primacy of drawing as a generator of, and guide toward, craftsmanship waned, eclectic architecture declined sharply. Wallace Neff is a prime example in this tragic tale of architectural triumph sliding into architectural disaster. The causes of this reversal in his fate and that of others should be sought in the changing nature of our society rather than in his personal qualities as an architect.

Note

1.   In the following section of sixteen pages, all material discussed is located in the Neff archive at the Huntington Library. The great Neff working drawings of the 1920s are signed by Clifton Hoskins, Edwin Westberg, Mark Ellsworth, Harry Balthesar, Everett Phipps Babcock, Robert Ainsworth, and others. Babcock and Ainsworth went on to establish important architectural practices of their own.

Fig. 79
San Fernando Mission Perspective,
1915.

T r a v e l   S k e t c h e s

SAN FERNANDO
JULY 3 1915

Wallace Neff's travel sketches are, first of all, indicative of his willingness to draw on a variety of sources. Though he is perhaps best known for his Spanish Revival work, such images appear only rarely in his extant sketches. Instead one finds a general interest in the rustic and vernacular. These sketches were both a source for, and an indication of, Neff's developing eclecticism.

The travel sketches are not exclusive in any sense. They comprise a great variety of building types and scales: rural, urban, monument, or fabric. In each case it is the sense of a whole that is recorded. Though details may feature prominently in the drawings, they are not detached from their context but exist as fundamental parts of the building fabric. Such an understanding of the relationship between the conception of the whole and the articulation of its parts pervaded Neff's architecture of the 1920s.

Light and texture are critical to these drawings. Neff recognized that they were integral to the making of important architecture. Light serves to model instead of simply illuminating the compositions. The sensual qualities of the drawings are developed by extending profile or outline to encompass the rendering of figures and surfaces. They embody a strong sense of movement, often by portraying symmetrical conditions in an asymmetrical manner.

As beautiful as these sketches are, they may not be distinguished as the work of an individual architect. Together with the drawings and photographs of Whittlesey, Requa, and others, they are part of a body of inspirational work which was broadly shared. Within this body, the act of recording was seen as an attempt to establish history as a continuity rather than as a means of isolating and abstracting. Through these drawings architects were not reviving but continuing traditions of place and form-making which were timeless.

Fig. 80
Farmer's House Perspective
Gruyères, France, 1914.

Fig. 81
Sketch of a Courtyard,
1920s.

P r e s e n t a t i o n   D r a w i n g s

Neff's presentation drawings, executed by his own hand and by others, evidence a great range of types and expressions. Beginning with shadow and texture, they evolve through several stages, including the introduction of color in an emblematic manner and the use of color as an abstract surface quality, and end with full color renderings.

Neff's own early courtyard sketch is a simple composition that begins with the figure of the building and its space. These are not delimited with line but are defined and rendered through the modulation of light and shadow. Appropriate detail is abstracted and added to the building through the same light and shadow. The space that results is populated, first with landscape elements that are

contained and controlled by the architecture in the form of pots or planters. Then animate objects, such as the cart or the chickens, are added to convey a sense of life and movement. The result is that the building is understood, through a fragment, as a complete idea; as a plastic composition activated through light; and as a vessel embodying and nurturing life.

The drawing of the Mary Pickford and Douglas Fairbanks Ranch, though depicting the whole building from some distance and making use of bold strokes of color, is remarkably similar to the courtyard sketch. Beginning with the same definition of form and texture through light and shadow, it places the building in a living landscape rather than placing landscape and life within the building. The forms of the house echo those of the mountains as the three roofs parallel the three peaks. Three birds hover above, completing the association. Color was added to the composition after the basic drawing was complete, in essence colorizing it. The bold strokes were applied in a systematic manner. First the roof was distinguished from the mountains and sky, then the building's openings—its connections to the landscape—were highlighted. Finally, the landscape elements that belong to the building itself were called out.

Color, in this drawing, is used in an emblematic manner. It further activates and articulates a set of forms already defined through strong contrasts of light and shadow. Not used to form the building, the color enlivens the building's forms instead.

The gouache image of a Bubble House in Mexico is a composition of abstract color shapes. Each shape, though treated as a plane, acts to define the modulation of light or shadow across a single surface. Gone is the definition of form through texture and with it any quality of material. However, context—landscape—remains a powerful compositional element. The strong shadow across the base of the drawing places the house in an urban environment—

a street with a row of buildings opposite. The two tall trees in the background imply a courtyard with an axial relationship with the doorway and connect the depths of the house with the street. Yet, the nature of the court remains as abstract as the image of the building as object.

The Arthur K. Bourne House watercolor attempts to combine full color rendering with the modulation of form and texture through light. Here color is not so much a quality of surface as it is of light and shadow. Material appears not as an implication of texture but as a real sensual presence. Once again the part conveys a sense of the whole.

As rich as the color work is, it represents a classic danger. Color in the gouache rendering has moved away from one of the many qualities of form to become its sole quality. The rendering ceases to discuss the nature of plastic form and becomes pure two-dimensional image. When color is approached in this manner, it tends to obscure the craft of building and issues such as profile, detail, and depth. It further alters the conception away from historical precedent and the whole of eclectic architecture toward a new architecture of pure and abstract imagery. The Bourne House drawing succeeds in that it resembles the watercolor travel sketches executed by architects on the Grand Tour. It does not sacrifice architectural issues to color but uses color to enhance the referential qualities and plasticity of the architectural composition.

Fig. 82
Bourne House,
Palm Springs,
rendering by Carl Oscar Borg.

Fig. 83
Sketch for Mary Pickford and Douglas Fairbanks Ranch Project,
1931.

Fig. 84
Reachi House Project.

Fig. 85
Fred Niblo House,
Beverly Hills, 1926,
foundation plan drawn by Mark W. Ellsworth.

W o r k i n g   D r a w i n g s

The most striking characteristics of the working drawings produced by Neff's office in the '20s are their extraordinary clarity and consistency. From a technical point of view, the hierarchy of notations and numbers, established by size and indicating degree of importance in the process of construction, is exquisite. The actual craft of producing such sheets of drawings is lost today.

From a philosophical point of view, the tendency to prescribe the experience of making buildings as place – through the moulding of material and space and the experience of living there – is ever-present. The sense of wholeness in these drawings is not limited to that of entirety nor to that of completeness but transcends and comprises both. In a world beset by the practice of working drawings as legal documents, the drawings of Neff's draughtsmen are works of art.

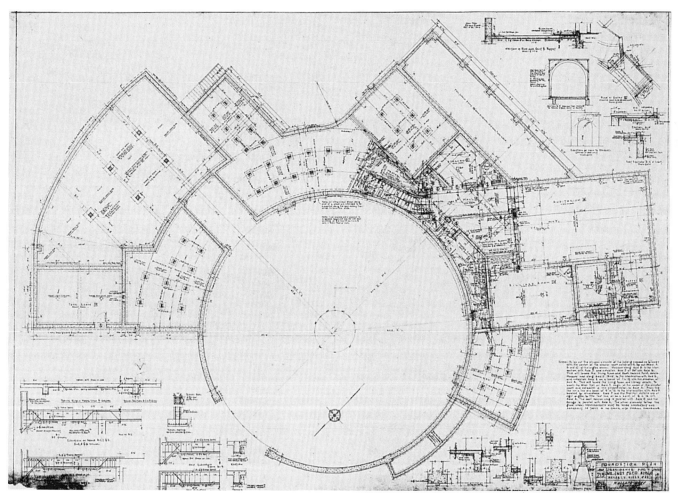

The **Fred Niblo House** foundation plan is expressive of the unusual form of a house conceived around a circular vehicle court. The geometry of the plan is accompanied by a series of explicit notations describing in detail the process of its layout step by step. The description is evocative of some kind of ancient ritual. Indeed, the foundation plan is given the veneration one might expect to be reserved for monumental Roman works and is drawn with equivalent strength. It expresses a tangible sense of respect for turning the earth, for occupying the ground.

Fig. 86
Niblo House,
foundation plan, detail.

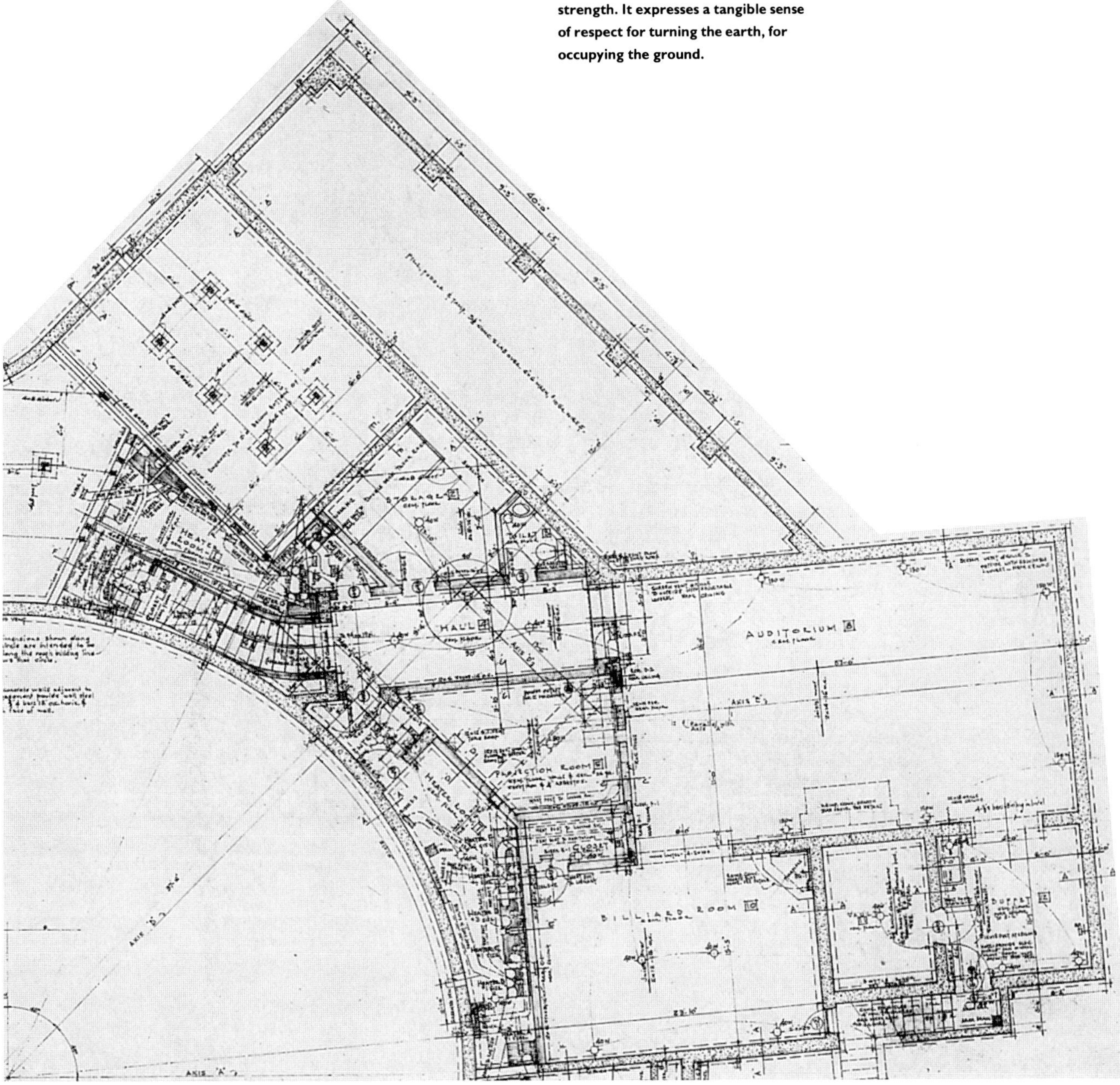

Fig. 87
Mr. and Mrs. King C. Gillette Ranch,
Calabasas, 1929,
plot plan and map of property,
drawn by J. G. R.

The enormous plot plan of the King C. Gillette Ranch describes the typical topographical aspects of such drawings, the configuration of the natural ground, and the spot elevations of its intersection with the house. In regard to locational issues the drawing is less than specific. It does not use dimensions to place the building relative to a property line or some other benchmark. Instead, through the intersection of the building form with the land forms, the intended relationship of house to nature is established. It further describes the whole experience of approaching and arriving at the house by car as well as the experience of being outdoors between the house and the natural landscape. Paradoxically, this drawing is drawn at ⅛" scale, which is the scale of all the other plans. It is as if by simply overlapping the common plans with the site plan, one could extend all of the qualities of being inside the house to its gardens and patios.

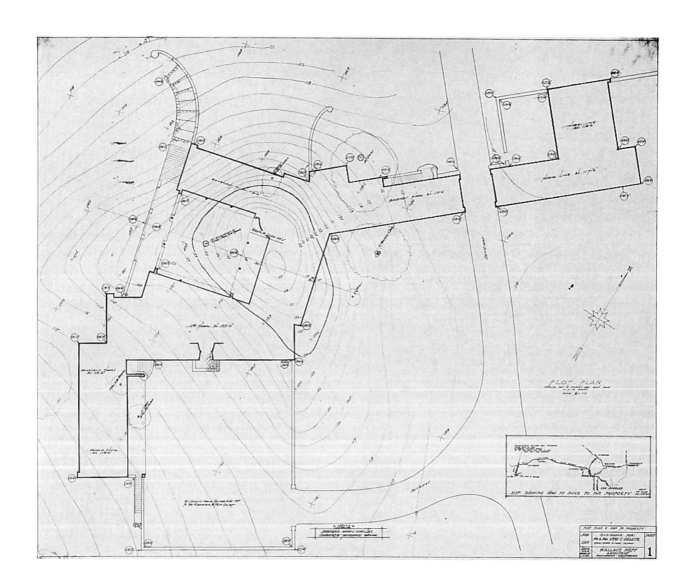

The plans for this same house are described primarily in terms of differentiating material from space. This is not unusual for such drawings. Here the rooms are carefully shaped and the poché is rendered in different thicknesses and kinds of materials in reference to the importance of each room. For instance, the public rooms are framed in deep composite walls, while the bathrooms on the second floor are subdivided by minimal stud walls. The prescription of qualities of place is absolute, but to the contractor, the method of execution remains discretionary.

Fig. 88
Gillette Ranch House,
first floor plan,
drawn by Arthur E. Fisk.

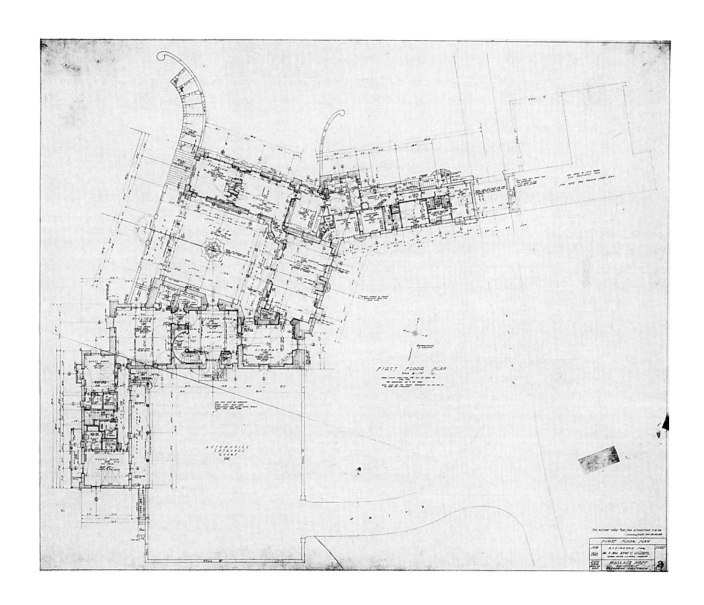

Fig. 89
Gillette Ranch House,
second floor and roof plans,
drawn by Arthur E. Fisk.

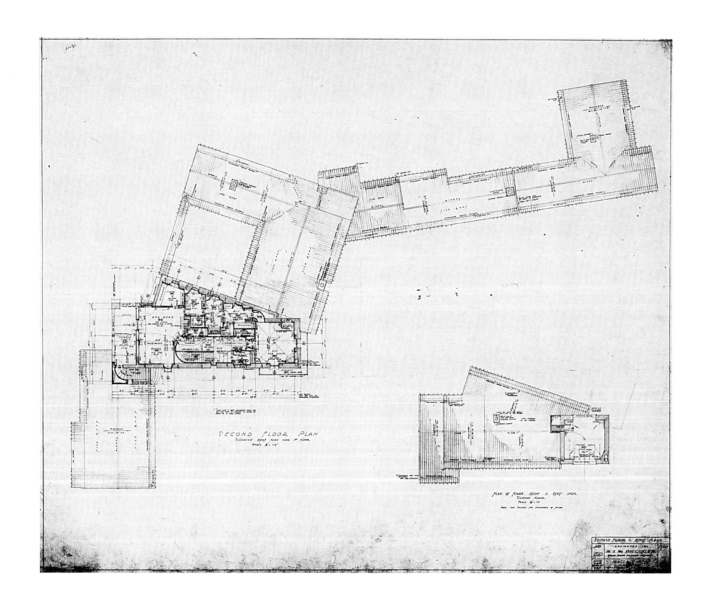

The overlap of information included in these drawings is extreme and speaks to the need for builders fully to understand the design intentions behind each line drawn. Likewise, it speaks to great skill on the part of the draughtsman in varying line weight and quality to provide a clear graphic language. Reflected ceiling plan notations, electrical fixture placements, dimensions and types of doors and windows, and paving and landscape items are all properly described and carefully overlapped. These drawings are a display of supreme confidence in the possibility of clear communication and correct building by conscientious craftsmen cognizant of their own trade and of others.

Fig. 90
Gillette Ranch House,
second floor and roof plans, detail.

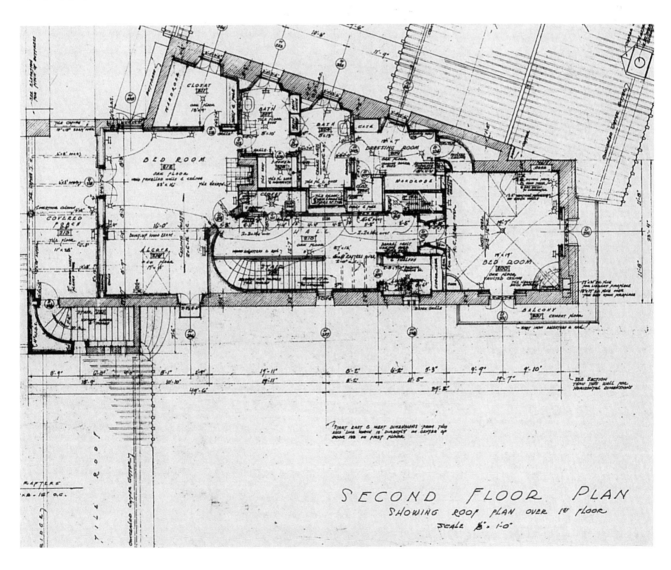

Fig. 91
Gillette Ranch House,
elevations, drawn by Edwin L. Westberg.

The exterior elevations of the Gillette Ranch House are selectively, not fully, rendered. The image of the house emerges tangibly, decisively, from these drawings. Not only is the building described in its overall configurations but its parts are highlighted in texture, pattern, and profile, detail or ornament, even in shadow. As in the case of the plans, there is no doubt whatsoever about the nature of the finished object or the qualities it will evoke.

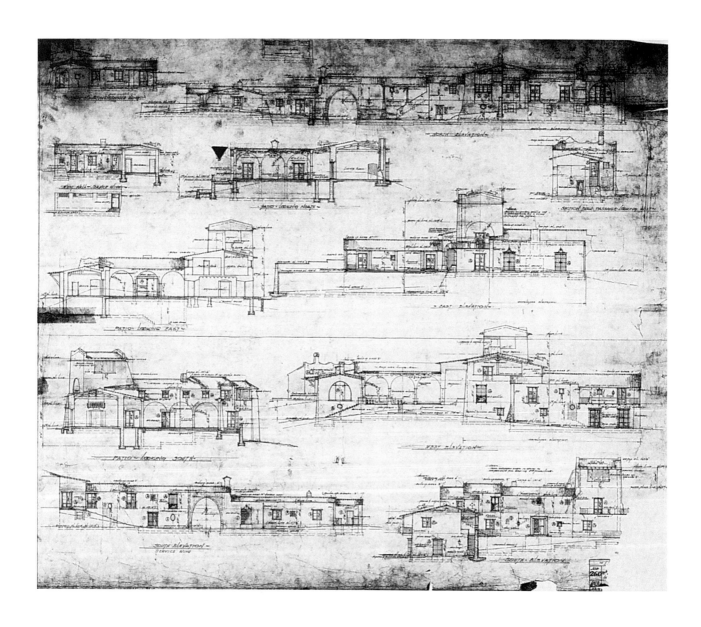

Fig. 92
Gillette Ranch House,
elevations, detail.

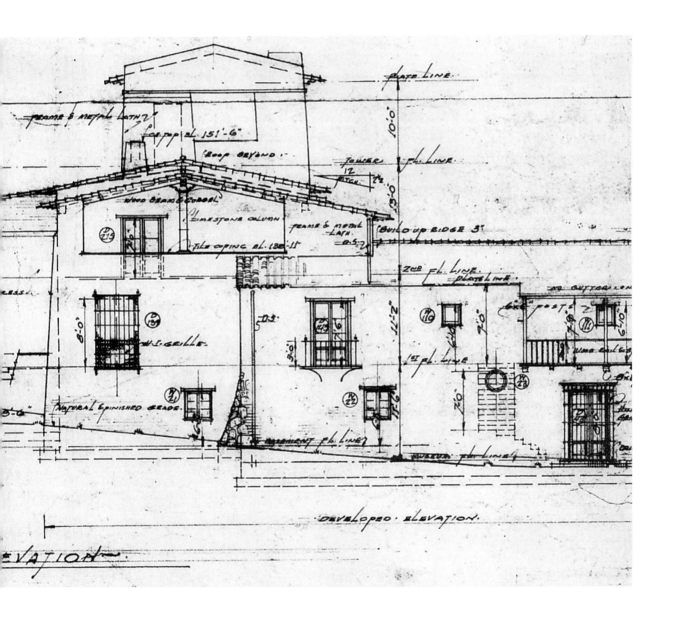

Fig. 93
Gillette Ranch House,
¼ scale interior elevations,
drawn by Mark W. Ellsworth.

Similarly, interior elevations describe rooms in full detail. Materials constituting surface, depth, and profile of various assemblies; the articulation of openings and the coordination of datums from wall to wall; and the correspondence of patterns and rhythms from ceiling to floor are all carefully orchestrated.

The millwork drawing illustrates the place of minor items of design in the body of a whole building. The degree of elaboration of doors and windows in terms of shape and pattern is evident here. Surprisingly, one encounters on this sheet the only large-scale details of moulding profiles. It appears that the demanding and vivid interior configurations and patterns for the whole house would have been executed by carpenters and plasterers on the basis of clear architectural description combined with common practice and sense.

The working drawings of the Neff
office before 1930 are typical of the
best of the national eclectic practices
of the period. They assume that
special objects and places should first
be constructed on paper and that the
building on paper was a powerful
enough inspiration and obligation to
the builder to ensure that he realized
it fully in situ.

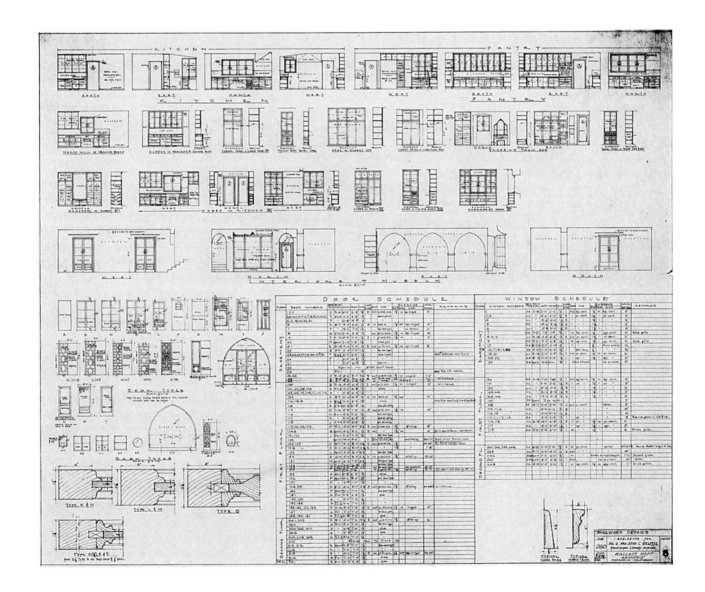

Fig. 95
Gillette Ranch House,
photograph by Padilla Studios.

P h o t o g r a p h s

Photography as a medium played a special role in the work of the Neff office before 1930. It was not merely descriptive in form and promotional in character but was a definite restatement of the ideas that generated the building in the first place. The two images of the King C. Gillette Ranch House are particularly instructive in this respect. They approximate the visual qualities of the perspective renderings of the Mary Pickford and Douglas Fairbanks Ranch project (fig. 83) and of an unidentified courtyard (fig. 81).

The panoramic photograph presents the house as a restatement of the mountains that are its background. The corner tower is the major vertical feature of the building and the pivot around which one circles in order to reach the entrance court. The gateway indicates the point of entry into the compound, and the large volumes of the building reveal its principal living spaces.

The photograph of the courtyard is equally expressive of the nature of the whole house. The strong contrasts of light and shadow that dominate the image establish a sense of depth and movement that lead the eye beyond the frame. Within and between the shadows are found the textures and profiles of the objects of dwelling which indicate the life of the place as a whole.

Together the photographs present the house, its gardens, and the larger landscape in a balance indicative of the will of the grand alliance of patrons, architects, and builders of the 1920s to endow the California countryside with the dignity of form and depth of history of its Mediterranean predecessor.

Fig. 96

Gillette Ranch House,
courtyard, photograph by Rolland W. Lee.

Fig. 97
**Mr. and Mrs.
Edwin D. Neff House,**
Pasadena, 1927.

BUILDINGS

by WALLACE NEFF,

FAIA

Jan Furey Muntz and

Margaret Meriwether

The Wallace Neff papers at the Huntington Library are far from complete, and unfortunately, there is no list of work from either his office records or his personal papers. Wallace Neff, Jr., provided a seminal list in his book (see Selected Bibliography, pp. 140–141), but more research is required to refine and expand it. We have continued this work but caution that the list provided here also is far from complete. It includes work never built, sole projects, joint projects, renovations, and additions; in most cases the dates given are building permit dates. Neff was frequently called back to homes he had designed to do additions and renovations. One of his most famous continous renovation projects, Douglas Fairbanks and Mary Pickford's Pickfair, frequently is incorrectly identified as Neff's original design.

We would appreciate any corrections or additions to this list. It will be revised periodically and will be available at the following locations: Pasadena City Hall, Pasadena Public Library, and the Huntington Library, San Marino.

Legend   **B**   Airform Construction (Balloon)

        R   Renovation/Addition

        D   Demolished

1919

Mr. and Mrs. Edwin D. Neff
*Santa Barbara: 1426 Alta Vista
Rd.*

1920

Kate Crane Gartz
*Altadena: 2015 – 2021 Lovilla
Lane (attributed)*

1922

Mac Blankenhorn
  Pasadena: 930 Arden Rd.

Thaddeus L. Up de Graff
  *Altadena: E. Mariposa
  Street – Project*

Thaddeus L. Up de Graff
  Altadena: 977 E. Mariposa St. **D**

Dr. Allan B. Kanavel
  Pasadena: 1015 S. El Molino Ave.

Marion M. Hill
  Pasadena: 822 S. El Molino Ave. **R**

H. George
  Altadena (attributed)

Mr. J. K. Baillie
  Pasadena: 1485 San Pasqual St.

1923

Clara M. Krug
  Pasadena: 830 S. Madison Ave.

Edward Drummond Libbey
  Ojai: Libbey Stables

Roy A. McDonald
  *La Cañada – Flintridge: Chevy
  Chase Dr./Berkshire*

Kate Crane Gartz
  Hollywood: Project

H. L. Delano
  Pasadena: 619 S. Hill Ave.

E. A. Kantell
  La Crescenta: 1823 Foothill Blvd.

Mr. and Mrs. Walter Hoffman
  Ventura: Rancho Casitas **D**

Mr. S. I. Allard
  Santa Barbara: Riviera District

Bryan Swearingen
  *Pasadena: 1549 E. California
  Blvd.*

Mrs. M. L. H. Walker
  *Pasadena: 1453 E. California
  Blvd.*

F. C. Van Deinse
  Pasadena: 329 Wigmore Drive

Joseph T. Penton
  Pasadena: Project

Mr. and Mrs. E. Wallace Neff
  Altadena: 1485 Mendocino Ave.

Ojai Valley Country Club
  Ojai: Country Club Rd.

Mr. and Mrs. Carroll Post
  Pasadena: 1235 S. Oakland Ave.

1924

Mr. and Mrs. Henry W. Schultz
  San Marino: 670 S. Allen Ave.

Mrs. Scoles
  *La Cañada – Flintridge: Nr.
  Flintridge Country Club*

Ojai Country Day School
  Ojai: Dormitory and Addition

St. Brigid Roman Catholic Church Rectory
  Los Angeles: 5214 S. Western Ave.

Pacific Southwest Realty Co.
  *Pasadena: Arcade at Colorado and
  Marengo – Project*

Mr. Chettford
  St. Augustine, Florida: Residence

Charles H. Cobb Building
  Altadena: 2416 N. Lake Ave.

Robert E. Hunter
  *Pasadena: 505 S. Orange Grove
  Blvd.* **R**

Carroll L. Post Building
  *Pasadena: East Colorado
  Blvd. – Project*

Dr. and Mrs. Phillip Schuyler Doane
  *San Marino: 1180 Shenandoah
  Rd.*

R. C. Kumler
  Pasadena: 1649 Lombardy Rd.

Mrs. R. C. Mankowski
Beverly Hills: 602 N. Maple Dr.

Horace M. Dobbins
Pasadena: Rodela del Sol — Jumbo
Hillside Development Project

Mr. and Mrs. Thomas I. O'Connor
Pasadena: 261 Wigmore Dr.

Dr. and Mrs. Milbank Johnson
Pasadena: 600 Burleigh Dr.
(R 1929)

Mrs. Frederick E. Newbury
Pasadena: 1550 San Pasqual St.

Dr. A. T. Newcomb
Pasadena: 1 Richland Pl.

Alice Cheny Smith
Pasadena: 1080 Prospect Blvd.

Mrs. Clara Force and Mrs. Marian
Gunnison
Pasadena: Studio and Garage —
1800 E. Mountain St.

George M. Buffum
Altadena: 711 W. Calaveras St.

Ethel Burr
Beverly Hills: 1022 Ridgedale Dr.

Thaddeus L. Up de Graff
Pasadena: 1590 E. California
Blvd.

Mr. and Mrs. Walter S. Young
Pasadena: 1040 Armada Dr.

Crowell and Katherine Beech
Pasadena: 790 Prospect Blvd.

Mrs. Wardwell
Pasadena: Hill Avenue
Residence — Project

Mr. and Mrs. A. P. Gates
Pasadena: 3 Richland Pl.

William Hays, Jr.
La Cañada — Flintridge

Mary P. Story
Pasadena: 470 Prospect Terr.

Miss Alice Beardsley
Pasadena: 527 Prospect Terr.

Colonel Bliss
Altadena (attributed)

Mrs. Henrietta B. Stowell
Pasadena: 707 S. Oakland Ave.

Burr-Moon Construction Co.
Beverly Hills: 1720 Chevy Chase
Dr.

Mr. and Mrs. Parker Toms
San Marino: 1861 Lombardy Rd.

1925

Mr. and Mrs. Arthur K. Bourne
San Marino: 2035 Lombardy Rd.
(R 1929)

Lincoln Mortgage Company
San Marino: 580 Berkeley Ave.

Lincoln Mortgage Company
San Marino: 589 Berkeley Ave.

Lincoln Mortgage Company
San Marino: 588 Berkeley Ave.

Lincoln Mortgage Company
San Marino: 581 Berkeley Ave.

Lincoln Mortgage Company
San Marino: 572 Berkeley Ave.

Lincoln Mortgage Company
San Marino: 549 Berkeley Ave.

Lincoln Mortgage Company
San Marino: 548 Berkeley Ave.

Mr. and Mrs. Shirley M. Hall
San Marino: 1300 Woodstock Rd.

Lincoln Mortgage Company
San Marino: 565 Berkeley Ave.

Lincoln Mortgage Company
San Marino: 564 Berkeley Ave.

Vernon Goodwin
Pasadena: 950 Arden Rd.

Saint Elizabeth's Church
Altadena: 1849 N. Lake Ave.

Lewis H. Starkey
>Pasadena: 1441 E. California
>Blvd.

Mrs. Grace A. Ohlmund
>Pasadena: 1465 E. Orange Grove
>Blvd.

C. B. Scoville, Jr.
>Pasadena: 120 Arroyo Blvd. **R**

Frances Marion and Fred Thomson
>Beverly Hills: Angelo Dr.

H. L. Winters
>La Cañada – Flintridge: 3924
>Alta Vista

Mr. and Mrs. J. Findley Torrence
>Pasadena: 195 La Vereda Rd.

Thaddeus L. Up de Graff
>San Marino: 615 S. Allen Ave.

Mr. and Mrs. Henry Stephen Boice
>Pasadena: 1057 Prospect Blvd.

Lawrence D. Macomber
>Pasadena: 940 Arden Rd.

Mr. and Mrs. Gaylord Martin
>San Marino: 1525 Wilson St.

Lincoln Mortgage Company
>San Marino: 596 Berkeley Ave.

D. M. Linnard
>Pasadena: Valley View, Huntington
>Circle Dr.

Mr. and Mrs. John G. McConnell
>La Cañada – Flintridge: 1966
>Lombardy Dr.

Morse and Gates (Ethel Guthrie)
>Pasadena: 1580 E. California
>Blvd.

Dr. John Willis Baer
>Montecito: 1424 La Vareda

Dr. and Mrs. Jarvis Barlow
>Sierra Madre: 200 N. Michillinda

J. Earlton Moore & Sons
>Beverly Hills: Project

Clara W. Burdette
>Pasadena: 121 N. Los Robles Ave.

Mrs. S. C. Fertig
>San Marino: 645 S. Allen Ave.

Marjorie Dobbins
>Pasadena: 535 Prospect Terr.

Ethel Burr
>Beverly Hills: 1800 Angelo Dr.

R. E. Campbell
>Beverly Hills Residence – Project

California Security Loan Corp.
>Pasadena: 315 – 325 E. Colorado
>Blvd. **D**

W. N. Caldwell
>Beverly Hills: 805 N. Linden Dr.

Mr. and Mrs. Frederick C. Fairbanks
>San Marino: 865 Orlando Rd.

A. R. Benedict
>Pasadena: 400 Ninita Pkwy.

1926

F. W. Stribling
>Pasadena: 550 S. Orange Grove
>Blvd.

Irving T. Bush
>Lake Wales, Florida: Residence

Edmund Goulding
>Beverly Hills: Benedict
>Canyon – Project

Fred Niblo
>Beverly Hills: 1330 Angelo Dr.

Forest Tucker
>South Pasadena: 530 Arroyo Sq.

Mr. and Mrs. George Jones
>South Pasadena: 511 Arroyo Sq.
>(attributed)

Keith Spalding
>Pasadena: 164 N. Euclid Ave.

Thaddeus L. Up de Graff
>Pasadena: 775 Holladay Rd.

Mr. and Mrs. William Neff
>Beverly Hills: 710 Walden Dr.

A. Stephen Vavra
>Los Angeles: Bel-Air Rd.

Dr. W. J. Stone
Pasadena: 1475 E. California
Blvd.

Mr. and Mrs. J. Crampton Anderson
Holmby Hills: 10162 Sunset Blvd.

J. E. Fenn
Beverly Hills: 1015 Roxbury Dr.
N.

A. M. G. Bertolotti
Beverly Hills: 814 N. Alpine Dr.

Walter S. McGilvray
Beverly Hills: 804 N. Alpine Dr.

Mr. and Mrs. Guy H. Witter
South Pasadena: 531 Arroyo Sq.
(attributed)

Mrs. Charlotte Pickford
Beverly Hills: 917 Benedict
Canyon Rd.

Carroll L. Post
San Marino: 861 Orlando Rd.

1927

A. J. Bayer
Beverly Hills: 628 Doheny Dr.

Saint Elizabeth's Church Rectory and
Convent
Altadena: 1849 N. Lake Ave.

Mr. and Mrs. Harry Culver
Cheviot Hills **D**

Mr. Edward W. Crellin
Pasadena: 1550 San Pasqual St. **R**

Mr. and Mrs. George O. Noble
Pasadena: 675 Burleigh Dr.

Mack Sennett
Los Angeles:
Hollywoodland – Project

Mr. and Mrs. Sidney L. Berg
Pasadena: 1290 Hillcrest Ave.

Mr. and Mrs. Wilbur H. Collins
Pasadena: 1522 Lombardy Rd.

Susanna Bixby Bryant
Santa Ana Canyon: Ranch **D**

Mr. and Mrs. Edwin D. Neff
Pasadena: 555 S. Orange Grove
Blvd.

Thaddeus L. Up de Graff
Pasadena: 795 Holladay Rd.

Charles A. Meyer
Los Angeles: Lafayette Park Tract

Colleen Moore
Los Angeles Residence – Project

Mrs. Nora Forthman
Los Angeles: 435 LaFayette Park
Pl.

Lawn Bowling Clubhouse
Pasadena: Central Park, S.
Raymond Ave. n. of Del Mar
(R 1929)

Lawrence G. McNeil
Beverly Hills: 619 N. Arden Dr.

1928

Mr. Erle M. Leaf
Los Angeles: 450 S. June St.

Edward L. Doheny, Jr.
Beverly Hills: Project

Mrs. Bertha Doerr (Mrs. Floyd Turner)
Pasadena: 1495 Orlando Rd.

R. R. Jones
San Marino: 1720 Ramiro Rd.

Mr. and Mrs. E. Wallace Neff
San Marino: 1883 Orlando Rd.

Mr. and Mrs. Robert Hunter
Pebble Beach

Mr. and Mrs. Charles H. Thorne
Pasadena: 114 Los Altos Dr.

Mr. and Mrs. King Vidor
Beverly Hills: 1636 Summit Ridge
Dr.

Mrs. J. W. Clune
Los Angeles: 2250 Chiselhurst
Dr. – Project

Thaddeus Libby Up de Graff
Pasadena: 755 Holladay Rd.

Mrs. Robert (Clara) Burdette
Pasadena: 1444 Wentworth Ave.

C. Harold Hopkins
Balboa

E. L. Petitfils
Los Angeles: 2441 N. Vermont Ave. **D**

Kate Crane Gartz
Palos Verdes: 304 Via Almar

1929

Mr. and Mrs. King C. Gillette
Calabasas: 26812 W. Mulholland Hwy.

John Gilbert
Beverly Hills R

Dr. and Mrs. Francis E. Browne
West Los Angeles: 721 Devon Ave.

Beatrix Eimer
Pasadena: 421 Olcott Pl. **D**

Mrs. E. W. Visscher
Brentwood: 515 N. Cliffwood Ave.

Mr. and Mrs. Edward L. Doheny
Santa Paula: Ferndale Ranch

Thaddeus L. Up de Graff
San Marino: 860 Oxford Rd.

Mr. and Mrs. Paul R. Richter
San Marino: 1221 Virginia Rd.

Mr. and Mrs. Norman Chandler
Los Angeles: Nottingham Rd.

Mrs. James K. Skinner
San Marino: 965 Orlando Rd.

Mr. and Mrs. Henry Grandin
Sierra Madre: Project

Mr. and Mrs. Henry S. I. Boice
Balboa: 1032 W. Ocean Front

Thaddeus L. Up de Graff
San Marino: 842 Oxford Rd.

Mr. and Mrs. Arthur K. Bourne
San Marino: 2035 Lombardy Rd. **R**

Neff-Ruppel Building
Pasadena: 180 E. California Blvd.

1930

S. L. Williams
San Marino: 860 Oxford Rd. **R**

Mary Pickford and Douglas Fairbanks
Beverly Hills: 1143 Summit Dr. **R**

Mr. and Mrs. William Goetz
Bel-Air: 303 Saint Pierre Rd.

Thaddeus L. Up de Graff
San Marino: 880 Oxford Rd.

Mr. and Mrs. Henry Bertolotti
San Marino: 2115 Orlando Rd.

1931

John Outchet
Bel-Air: 70 Bel-Air Rd.

Mr. and Mrs. LeRoy Sanders
Pasadena: 1525 Orlando Rd. **R**

Mr. and Mrs. Clark B. Millikan
Pasadena: 1500 Normandy Dr.

Sol Wurtzel
Bel-Air: 10539 Bellagio Rd.

J. B. Keating
Pasadena: Lombardy Rd. and Madre St.

1932

John Lewis Neff
Pasadena: 3300 Yorkshire Rd.

Mary Pickford and Douglas Fairbanks
Rancho Santa Fe: Rancho Zorro – Project

Dr. and Mrs. R. C. Hall
La Mesa

Doheny Repository Throne
Los Angeles: Saint Vincent de Paul Church

Mr. and Mrs. Arthur K. Bourne
Glendora: 820 Verano Dr.

1933

Arthur K. Bourne
Palm Springs: 486 S. Patencio Rd.

Mr. and Mrs. Frederick March
    Beverly Hills: 1026 Ridgedale Dr.

Mr. and Mrs. James R. Page
    Los Angeles: 354 S. Windsor Blvd.
    R

1934

Honeymoon Cottage
    *Los Angeles: Wilshire Blvd. –
    moved to 1330 S. Rimpau Blvd.*

Mr. and Mrs. Edward L. Doheny
    Los Angeles: 7 and 11 Chester Pl.
    R

1935

Robert Garner, Jr.
    San Marino: 937 Avondale Rd.

1936

Mr. and Mrs. Gene Markey (Joan Bennett)
    Holmby Hills: 515 Mapleton Dr.

Mr. and Mrs. Robert E. Brigham
    Bel-Air: 10408 Sunset Blvd.

Amelita Galli-Curci
    Westwood: 201 Tilden Ave.

Mr. and Mrs. Lawrence Beilenson
    Hollywood: N. Gramercy Pl.

Dr. and Mrs. Pressman
    Holmby Hills: 615 N. Faring Rd.
    R

Dr. and Mrs. Stanley Imerman
    Beverly Hills: 1143 Tower Rd.

1937

Mr. and Mrs. Darryl Zanuck
    Santa Monica: Pacific Coast Hwy.

Mr. and Mrs. Darryl Zanuck
    Beverly Hills: Project

King Vidor
    Beverly Hills: 1140 Tower Rd. D

Claudette Colbert
    Beverly Hills: 615 Faring Rd. R

Clarence Brown
    Los Angeles: Stokes Canyon

1938

Mr. and Mrs. George Miller
    Bel-Air: 10615 Bellagio Rd.

Mr. and Mrs. Charles Chaplin
(Paulette Goddard)
    Beverly Hills: Project

Herman Hirsch
    Beverly Hills: 1050 Angelo Dr. D

1939

Louis O'Bryan
    Arcadia: 1225 Rodeo Rd.

Mr. and Mrs. F. N. Cole
    Beverly Hills: 1138 Tower Rd. D

Snow Valley Winter Sports Lodge
    San Bernardino County Project

Edward L. Doheny Memorial Library
    Camarillo: Saint John's Seminary

Joseph Schenck
    Snow Valley: Project

Mr. and Mrs. Henry F. Haldeman
    Beverly Hills: 10000 Sunset Blvd.

1940

Doheny Memorial House of Studies
    *Washington, D.C.: Catholic
    University*

Mrs. W. R. Osburn
    Los Angeles: 516 S. Rimpau Blvd.

Averell Harriman
    *Sun Valley, Idaho: Ski
    Lodge – Project*

Mr. and Mrs. William Goetz
    Santa Monica: 522 Ocean Front

Amelita Galli-Curci
    Lake Arrowhead: Cottage

Mr. and Mrs. Walter Hoffman
    Beverly Hills: 441 Oakhurst Dr. D

Mr. and Mrs. Warren B. Duff
  Brentwood: 13525 Lucca Dr.

1941

Pneumatic Form – First Patent Application
  *Washington, D.C.: Serial No.
  386727* **B**

Mrs. Ivy Merton
  Pacific Palisades: 1325 Lucca Dr.
  R

Mr. and Mrs. Walter Reisch
  Bel-Air: 332 Bel-Air Rd.

Defense Housing Corporation
  *Falls Church, Virginia: Horseshoe
  Hill* **B**

1942

Goodyear Litchfield Park
  *Litchfield Park Arizona: Desert
  Housing Colony and Grain
  Storage* **B, D**

Parachute Plant Bomb Shelter
  Vernon: Cole of California

Stage Houses, Polaris Flight Academy
  Lancaster: Project **B**

1943

Pacific Linen Supply
  Los Angeles: 901 – 907 E. 8th St.
  B, D

1944

Engineering School Classrooms, Loyola
University
  *Los Angeles: W. 80th and Loyola
  Blvd.* **B**

1945

Housing Project
  Brazil: Rio de Janeiro **B**

Theater Project
  South Africa: Johannesburg **B**

Mr. and Mrs. William Neff (Mina Braly)
  San Marino: 568 Los Arboles Ln.

Mr. and Mrs. Sam Jaffe
  Beverly Hills: 1144 Alta Dr.

Capt. and Mrs. James Young
  Westwood: 11444 Thurston Cir.

Circa 1945

Mr. and Mrs. Robert Taylor
  Beverly Hills – Project

1946

Dr. Andrew Neff
  Pasadena: 1097 S. Los Robles Ave.
  B

Sullivan Hall and Huesman Hall, Loyola
University
  *Los Angeles: 710 W. 80th and
  Loyola Blvd.*

Myrtle Hornstein
  *Beverly Hills: 9531 Hidden Valley
  Rd.*

Monastery of the Angels
  Hollywood: 1977 Carmen Pl. **R**

Mrs. Thomas Ince
  *South Pasadena: 360 Alta Vista
  Ave.* **B, D**

Loyola Memorial Gymnasium, Loyola
University
  *Los Angeles: W. 80th and Loyola
  Blvd.*

1947

School Complex
  Mexico: Mexico City **B**

Bureau of Indian Affairs Housing
  Washington, D.C. Project **B**

1948

Mr. and Mrs. Leonard Firestone
  Beverly Hills: 1014 Laurel Ln. **R**

Dr. and Mrs. John Haigh
  *San Marino: 1173 San Marino
  Ave.*

Alan Ladd
  Holmby Hills **R**

Mr. and Mrs. Harry Kunin
  *Holmby Hills: 10713 Brooklawn
  Dr.*

Amelita Galli-Curci
  Rancho Santa Fe: Los Plaridaris

1949

Kellogg Gymnasium
Claremont: Pomona College

Harry Cranston
Pasadena: 1437 Hillcrest Ave. **R**
(attributed)

Kadena Air Force Base
Okinawa – Project **B**

Hulett Clinton Merritt
Pasadena: 99 Terrace Dr. **R**
(attributed)

Dr. and Mrs. John Tragerman
Los Feliz: 2300 W. Live Oak Dr.

1950

Airform – One Thousand Structures
French West Africa (Senegal): Dakar **B**

Altar for Precious Blood Church
Los Angeles: 435 Occidental Blvd.

Thomas Ince Memorial Hospital
Twentynine Palms – Project

Mr. and Mrs. Shirley Burden
Beverly Hills: 1026 Ridgedale Dr. **R**

Edmunds Student Union
Claremont: Pomona College **R**

Myron Kunin
Bel-Air: 10550 Dolcedo Wy.

1951

Bergin
Beverly Hills: 208 S. Bedford Dr.

Leonard Chudacoff
Beverly Hills: 1150 Tower Rd.

Mr. and Mrs. Edward L. Doheny
Capistrano Beach **R**

1952

Conrad Hilton
Beverly Hills: 9970 Santa Monica Blvd. **R**

Annie M. Forthman
Trancas Beach, Malibu: 31316 Broad Beach Rd.

Nora Forthman
Trancas Beach, Malibu: 31310 Broad Beach Rd.

Eleanor Boardman
Los Angeles: 1007 N. Beverly Dr. **R**

Manuel Reachi
Mexico: Ensenada – Project

Rella and John Factor
Beverly Hills: 1184 Loma Linda Dr.

Bendix
Beverly Hills: 620 Linden Drive N. **R**

Mr. and Mrs. H. T. (Madeline) Boyer
Trancas Beach, Malibu: 31302 Broad Beach Rd.

1953

Airform Grain Storage
Jordan: Amman **B**

1954

Manuel Reachi
Ensenada, Mexico: Project

1955

Manresa Jesuit Chapel
Azusa: 18337 E. Foothill Blvd.

S. W. Barrett
San Marino: 1040 Oak Grove Ave. **R**

Hal Wallace
Holmby Hills: 515 Mapleton Dr. **R**

Adler
Beverly Hills: 703 N. Cañon

1956

Mr. and Mrs. Edgar Richards
Rancho Mirage

Wine Storage
Portugal: Bemfica **B**

Mr. and Mrs. George Miller
Palm Springs: Rock 10 – Smoke Tree Ranch

Cary Grant
Bel-Air: 10615 Bellagio Rd. **R**

Mr. and Mrs. Edgar Richards
> *Los Angeles: 2754 Monte Mar*
> *Terr.*

Groucho Marx
> *Trousdale Estates, Beverly Hills:*
> *1083 Hillcrest Rd.*

John Woodward
> *Hancock Park: 200 S. Hudson*
> *Ave.*

Harpo Marx
> *Palm Springs: El Rancho Harpo*

1957

Al Marshall
> *Coachella Valley: 554 S. Van Ness*

Cary Grant
> *Palm Springs: 928 Avenidas*
> *Palmas* **R**

Zeppo Marx
> *Palm Springs: Wonder Estates*

Gummo Marx
> *Beverly Hills: 1076 Marilyn Dr.*

Leo S. Bing
> *Beverly Hills: 380 Carolwood Dr.*
> **R**

Jim Hughes
> *Los Angeles: 836 S. Rimpau Blvd.*

Dr. and Mrs. Francis E. Browne
> *Bel-Air: 811 Strada Vecchia Rd.*

Mrs. Anna Bing Arnold
> *Beverly Hills: 1270 Shadow Hill*
> *Wy.*

Willard W. Keith
> *Beverly Hills: 1230 Laurel Wy.*

Mr. and Mrs. Sam Hayden
> *Beverly Hills: 419 Robert Ln.*

1958

Samuel B. Gerry
> *Beverly Hills: 413 Robert Ln.*

1960

Louise G. Hahn
> *Beverly Hills: 1054 Shadow Hill*
> *Wy.*

1961

Mr. and Mrs. Arthur Gilbert
> *Los Angeles: Heather Rd.*

Cecil Virncoff
> *Los Angeles: 1255 N. Wetherly*
> *Dr.*

Mr. and Mrs. Ralph Chandler
> *Hancock Park: 105 S. Rossmore*
> *Ave.* **R**

Edward L. Doheny Memorial Library
> *Camarillo: Saint John's Seminary* **R**

Red Skelton
> *Rancho Mirage* **R**

1962

Dr. and Mrs. Burton (Pat) Fletcher
> *Bel-Air: 11100 Chalon Rd.*

Roy and Dorothy Eaton
> *Goleta: 7142 Del Monte Dr.*

Casa de Guadalupe
> *Los Angeles: 9635 Santa Monica*
> *Blvd.*

Roy and Dorothy Eaton
> *Santa Barbara: 800 Via*
> *Hierba — Hope Ranch*

Tony Curtis
> *Los Angeles* **R**

Pineapple Beach Club
> *Saint Thomas, Virgin Islands:*
> *Charlotte Amalie* **B**

Mr. and Mrs. Peter Hummel
> *Reno, Nevada: 2140 Green Tree*

1963

Amelita Galli-Curci
> *La Jolla: 2456 Calle del Oro*

134

Frank Homy
Los Angeles: 125 N. La Brea

1965

Mr. and Mrs. Verne H. Winchell
San Marino – Project

1966

Gummo Marx
Palm Desert: 37 – 661 Golf Cir.

1967

Mr. and Mrs. Eugene Allen
Bel-Air: 110 N. Rockingham Ave.

Mr. and Mrs. John Elliot
Maui, Hawaii: Hana

Mr. and Mrs. Howard Wilson
*Los Angeles: 2050 Mandeville
Canyon Rd.*

1968

Mrs. Phillip Reed
Los Angeles: Bel Air Rd.

Mr. and Mrs. Stanley Hahn
Pasadena: 72 Los Altos Dr.

1969

Dr. and Mrs. Henry Singleton
Holmby Hills: 384 Delfern Dr.

Mr. and Mrs. Robert K. Straus
*Santa Barbara: 4377
Marina – Hope Ranch*

1970

Tom Harmon
Beverly Hills – Project **R**

1972

Mr. and Mrs. Patrick Frawley
Holmby Hills: Club View Dr. **R**

1973

Elizabeth Hay Bechtel
*Montecito: Birnam Woods
Guest House*

1975

Elizabeth Hay Bechtel
*Montecito: Birnam Woods
Residence*

Dr. and Mrs. Francis E. Browne
*Irvine Ranch: 18 Cypress Point
Ln.*

Date Unknown

Louis Golan
Beverly Hills: Calle Vista Dr.

Meyberg
Los Angeles: 556 S. Rimpau Blvd.
R

Mervyn LeRoy
Bel-Air: 332 Saint Cloud Rd.

Roy Eaton
*Los Angeles: Forest Lawn
Mausoleum*

Allen D'Dal
Hidden Valley – Project

Gadbois
*Cheviot Hills: Hillcrest Country
Club*

S. K. Eisen
Beverly Hills – Project

Mosque
Turkey – Project **B**

Mr. and Mrs. Walter S. Young
Newport Beach – Project

Gas Stations for Standard Oil Company
Los Angeles

Saint Mary's Academy
Ventura: Convent

Mary Pickford
Mausoleum – Project

Downtown College, Loyola University
*Los Angeles: 11th St. and Grand
Ave. – Project*

Farm Workers' Housing
California – Project **B**

Fig. 98
Mr. and Mrs.
Robert K. Straus House,
Santa Barbara, 1969.

EXHIBITION

ACKNOWLEDGMENTS

Jay Belloli

The exhibition *Wallace Neff, 1895–1982: The Romance of Regional Architecture* was presented by the Virginia Steele Scott Gallery from May 6 through September 4, 1989, and was funded by grants from the National Endowment for the Arts, Washington, D.C., a Federal agency, and the Pasadena Gallery of Contemporary Arts. The exhibition could not have taken place without the ongoing support of Dr. Robert R. Wark, Curator of Art Collections at the Huntington Library and Art Gallery, and I am grateful for his encouragement. Susan Danly, former Associate Curator of American Art, provided assistance in developing the exhibition concept. Amy Meyers, Associate Curator of American Art, coordinated the project for the Huntington and contributed her time, expertise, and enthusiasm. Jacqueline Dugas, Administrative Associate, assisted with numerous details, and Eric Lutz, Preparator, spent long hours matting and framing the drawings and photographs for the show. The Huntington is grateful to Richard Dobbins for lending an important drawing to the exhibition.

I would like to convey my gratitude to the other members of the guest curatorial committee for the exhibition: Alson Clark, Architectural Collection Advisor at the Huntington, whose many years of research into Wallace Neff's achievement have been essential to this project; Jan Furey Muntz, a practicing architect and Lecturer in Architecture, Woodbury University; Stefanos Polyzoides, partner in the firm de Bretteville and Polyzoides and Associate Professor of Architecture, University of Southern California; and Charles Calvo, a Ph.D. candidate at the University of California, Los Angeles.

WORKS in the EXHIBITION

All works collection of the Huntington unless listed otherwise.

1.
Street View Perspective
Gruyères, France, 1914
Pencil on paper, 11″ × 7⅝″

2.
Farmer's House Perspective
Gruyères(?), 1914
Pencil on paper, 6″ × 6¾″

3.
San Fernando Mission Perspective
1915
Pencil on paper, 7¾″ × 11″

4.
Sketch of a Courtyard
1920s
Pencil on paper, 13¼″ × 12¼″

5.
Mr. and Mrs. Edwin D. Neff House
Santa Barbara, 1919, Interior
Black-and-white photograph, 8″ × 10″
Photographer unknown

6.
Edward Drummond Libbey Stables
Ojai, 1923, Exterior with Tower
Color photograph of rendering, 8″ × 10″

7.
Libbey Stables
East and West Elevations, 1923
Pencil on tracing paper, 30″ × 38½″
Drawn by Wallace Neff

8.
Ojai Valley Country Club
1923−24, Exterior
Black-and-white photograph, 8″ × 10″
Photograph by Margaret Craig

9.
**Frances Marion and
Fred Thomson House**
Beverly Hills, 1923−24
Rendering reproduced on cover of California
Southland *(August 1925), 8½″ × 8″*
Rendering by Norman Kennedy

10.
Marion and Thomson House
Entrance with Coats of Arms
Black-and-white photograph, 8″ × 10″
Photograph by William M. Clarke

11.
Mr. and Mrs. Parker Toms House
San Marino, 1924
Color photograph, 8″ × 10″
Photograph by Rolland W. Lee

12.
**Dr. and Mrs. Phillip Schuyler
Doane House**
San Marino, 1924
Color photograph, 8″ × 10″
Photograph by Rolland W. Lee

13.
Mr. and Mrs. Arthur K. Bourne House
San Marino, 1925
Black-and-white photograph, 8″ × 10″
Photograph by Rolland W. Lee

14.
Bourne House
Facade
Black-and-white photograph, 10″ × 8″
Photograph by William M. Clarke

15.
**Horace M. Dobbins
Hillside Development**
Project, Pasadena, 1924, Rendering
Gouache on paper, 16½″ × 34″ (with mat)
Collection of Mr. Richard Dobbins, Pasadena

16.
H. L. Delano House
Pasadena, 1923
Color photograph, 8″ × 10″
Photograph by Grey Crawford

17.
Fred Niblo House
Beverly Hills, 1926, Foundation Plan
Pencil on tracing paper, 34″ × 47″
Drawn by Mark W. Ellsworth

18.
Niblo House
First Floor Plan
Pencil on tracing paper, 34″ × 48″
Drawn by W. De H.

19.
Niblo House
Elevations
Pencil on tracing paper, 34″ × 48″
Drawn by Clifton R. Hoskins

20.
Niblo House
Sections and Plot Plan
Pencil on tracing paper, 34″ × 42″
Drawn by Arthur E. Fisk

21.
Niblo House
Aerial View
Color photograph, 8″ × 10″
Photograph by Louis Bruhnke

22.
Mr. and Mrs. George O. Noble House
Pasadena, 1927
Color photograph, 8″ × 10″
Photograph by Rolland W. Lee

23.
Noble House
Entrance Hall
Color photograph, 10″ × 8″
Photograph by Rolland W. Lee

24.
**Berkeley Avenue Speculative House
Lincoln Mortgage Company**
San Marino, 1927
Color photograph, 8″ × 10″
Photograph by Rolland W. Lee

Fig. 99
Neff-Ruppel Building,
Pasadena, 1929.

S E L E C T E D

B I B L I O G R A P H Y

The most complete bibliography on Wallace Neff is published in Wallace Neff, Jr., ed., and Alson Clark, *Wallace Neff: Architect of California's Golden Age* (Santa Barbara, 1986).

"Airform House for a Desert Colony." *Architectural Record* 96 (July 1946): p. 113.

Allen, Harris. "Adventures in Architecture." *Pacific Coast Architect* 32 (September 1927): p. 9.

————. "An Artist in Adobe." *Pacific Coast Architect* 26 (August 1924): p. 6.

"A New House on Lombardy Road." *California Southland* 7 (October 1925): p. 22.

"Balloon Houses Designed for Defense Workers Bloom Under Virginia Trees." *Life* (December 1, 1941): pp. 34–35.

"Building for Defense." *Architectural Forum* 73 (March 1941): pp. 3, 174.

"Building for Defense: Ballyhooed Balloon." *Architectural Forum* 75 (December 1941): p. 421.

Carpenter, Warwick. "Cottage for Two." *American Home* (November 1934): p. 23.

Gebhard, David, and Robert Winter. *A Guide to Architecture in Los Angeles and Southern California.* Salt Lake City, 1977.

Glass, Charles Ray. "The Return of the Spanish Hacienda." *Arts and Decoration* 30 (January 1927): p. 40.

Gloag, John. *Men and Buildings.* London, 1950: p. 233.

————, ARIBA, and Grey Wornum, FRIBA. *House Out of Factory.* London, 1946: pp. 17–19.

"Honeymoon Cottage." *American Architect* 146/2631 (March 1935): p. 72.

"Honeymoon Cottage." *California Arts and Architecture* 46 (August 1934): p. 23.

Kelley, H. Roy. "The California Situation from the Architect's Point of View." *Pacific Coast Architect* 33 (November 1928): p. 11.

Kelley, H. Roy. "The California Situation from the Architect's Point of View." *Pacific Coast Architect* 33 (November 1928): p. 11.

Moore, Charles, Peter Becker, and Regula Campbell. *The City Observed: Los Angeles*. New York, 1984.

Neff, Wallace. *Architecture of Southern California: A Selection of Photographs, Plans and Scale Details from the Work of Wallace Neff, FAIA*. Chicago, 1964.

Neff, Wallace, Jr., ed., and Alson Clark. *Wallace Neff: Architect of California's Golden Age*. Santa Barbara, 1986.

Newcomb, Rexford. *Mediterranean Domestic Architecture in the United States*. Cleveland, 1928.

————. "Personality in Regional Architecture." *Western Architect* 35 (February 1926): pp. 22–23.

————. *Spanish-Colonial Architecture in the United States*. New York, 1937.

Seares, M. Urmy. "The California House in Florida." *California Southland* 7 (September 1926): p. 8.

Wallace Neff Papers. Huntington Library, San Marino.